JOHN CHANDLER
University of Nottin
research work in in
lecturer in Chemist
College and now
Technical College. He is also a
and A-level Chemistry courses for Wolsey Hall, Oxford.

RICK WILKINSON is a graduate of the University of Southampton. He gained a Ph.D. for his research work in Organic Chemistry. He has lectured in Physics and Chemistry at Basingstoke Technical College and is now Principal of Winchester Tutorial College.

key facts

Worked Examples

APPLIED MATHEMATICS, E. M. Peet, B.Sc.

BIOLOGY, A. G. Toole, B.Sc.

CHEMISTRY, J. E. Chandler, B.Sc.
and R. J. Wilkinson, Ph.D.

ECONOMICS, R. Maile, B.A.

GEOGRAPHY, C. Lines, M.Sc.

PHYSICS, G. M. George, B.Sc.

PURE MATHEMATICS, R. A. Parsons, B.Sc.
and A. G. Dawson, B.Sc.

PURE AND APPLIED MATHEMATICS,
R. A. Parsons, B.Sc. and A. G. Dawson, B.Sc.

GCE A-Level

Chemistry

J. E. Chandler, B.Sc.
and
R. J. Wilkinson, Ph.D.

key facts

Published by Charles Letts Books Ltd
London, Edinburgh and New York

This book is sold subject to the condition that it shall not, by way of trade or otherwise, be lent, re-sold, hired out, or otherwise circulated without the publisher's prior consent in any form of binding or cover other than that in which it is published and without a similar condition including this condition being imposed on the subsequent purchaser.

Published 1983 by Charles Letts Books Ltd
Diary House, Borough Road, London SE1 1DW

1st edition, 1st impression
© Charles Letts Books Ltd
Made and printed by Charles Letts (Scotland) Ltd
ISBN 0 85097 553 0

Contents

Introduction

The aim of this book is to provide worked examples of questions found in the most recent G.C.E. A level papers of both traditional and Nuffield Chemistry.

Most examination boards now set three types of theory paper: Multiple Choice, Structured and Long Answer.

Questions are included on all sections of the major syllabuses and readers are advised to check what topics they require.

In Chapter 1 we have included the multiple-choice questions most frequently encountered. The remaining chapters feature structured questions which have a mark allocation against each part and long answer questions which either involve calculations or are comprised of many parts. We have not included any essay questions.

The chapters have been arranged to follow the order of the *Chemistry A-level Passbook* also by the authors.

The questions have been chosen from recent past papers of the Associated Examining Board Syllabus 2 (A.E.B.), the Southern Universities Joint Board (S.U.J.B.) and the University of London Schools Examination Board traditional syllabus (L) and Nuffield syllabus (NUFF). We are most grateful to these examining boards for granting us permission to reproduce their questions.

The answers are entirely those of the authors. The A.E.B., S.U.J.B. and London University Schools Examination Board accept no responsibility whatsoever for the accuracy or method of working in the answers given.

All physical data has been taken from the *Chemistry Data Book* by Stark & Wallace. Some examination boards do not give data with the question but allow this book or the Nuffield Data Book to be taken into the exam.

Chapter 1

Multiple-choice questions

Section I

Directions Each group of questions below consists of five lettered headings followed by a list of numbered questions. For each numbered question select the one heading which is most closely related to it.

Each heading may be used once, more than once, or not at all.

Questions 1–6 concern the following types of structure:

A Giant structure of ions.
B Giant structure of atoms.
C Widely spaced molecules.
D Widely spaced atoms.
E Molecular crystals.

Select from A to E, the structure possessed by each substance below, at room temperature and atmospheric pressure.

1 Naphthalene.
2 Carbon monoxide.
3 Graphite.
4 Silicon(IV) oxide.
5 Helium.
6 Caesium chloride.

Questions 7–12 concern the following compounds:

A CH_2OH
$|$
CH_2OH

B $CH_3.CHCl.COOH$

C 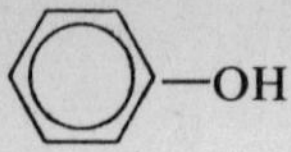

D 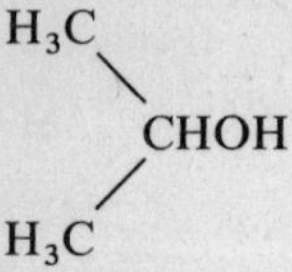

E 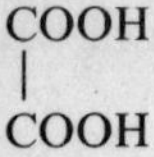

Select, from A to E above, the compound that:

7 yields a poisonous gas on dehydration.

8 on careful oxidation with acidified potassium dichromate(VI) gives another compound on the above list.

9 reacts with aqueous sodium hydroxide, but NOT with aqueous sodium carbonate.

10 forms esters readily when treated with acid chlorides, but NOT when treated with acids.

11 readily forms tri-iodomethane (CHI_3) on treatment with iodine and alkali.

12 when prepared by normal chemical methods, consists of a mixture of two isomers.

Questions 13–17 concern the following hydrocarbons:

A Ethyne (acetylene).
B Ethene (ethylene).
C Methane.
D Benzene.
E Cyclohexane.

Select, from A to E above, the hydrocarbon that:

13 is a useful raw material in the manufacture of ammonia.

14 produces a red precipitate when bubbled through ammoniacal copper(I) chloride solution.

15 is a liquid at 20°C and does not combine with hydrogen even in the presence of nickel.

16 is formed when ethanol vapour is passed over aluminium oxide at 200°C.

17 is a liquid at 20°C and reacts in two different ways with chlorine, depending on the conditions.

Section II

Questions 18–24

Directions For each of the questions below, ONE or MORE of the responses given are correct. Decide which of the responses is (are) correct. Then choose:

A if only 1, 2 and 3 are correct.
B if only 1 and 3 are correct.
C if only 2 and 4 are correct.
D if only 4 is correct.
E if some other response, or combination of responses, of those given is correct.

Directions summarized				
A 1, 2, 3 only	B 1, 3 only	C 2, 4 only	D 4 only	E Some other response or combination of responses

18 Which masses of gas would occupy about 6ℓ at room temperature and pressure? (1 mole of a gas occupies 24ℓ at room temperature and pressure. Relative atomic masses: H = 1; C = 12; O = 16; S = 32; Ar = 40.)

1 8.5 g of hydrogen sulphide.

2 4 g of oxygen.
3 11 g of carbon dioxide.
4 20 g of argon.

19 At room temperature, ethanoic acid (acetic acid) will react with:

1 lithium tetrahydridoaluminate(III) (lithium aluminium hydride, $LiAlH_4$).
2 phosphorus pentachloride (PCl_5).
3 sodium carbonate (Na_2CO_3).
4 acidified potassium manganate(VII) ($KMnO_4$).

20 The following are the electronic configurations of four metal ions having the charges indicated. Which ion(s) is/are colourless in aqueous solution?

1 (Ar) +2.
2 (Ar)$3d^5$ +3.
3 (Ar)$3d^{10}$ +1.
4 (Ar)$3d^{10}$ +2.

21 Correct statements about the Group II elements:
magnesium
calcium
strontium
barium

include that they ALL:

1 react with boiling water.
2 form oxides that are strongly basic.
3 have carbonates that are insoluble in water.
4 have sulphates that are insoluble in water.

22 The equation for the reaction between propanone and iodine is:

$$CH_3.CO.CH_3(aq) + I_2(aq) \longrightarrow CH_3.CO.CH_2I(aq) + H^+(aq) + I^-(aq)$$

The reaction is catalysed by hydrogen ions and the order with respect to iodine is zero.
What can be deduced from this information?

1 The hydrogen ions decrease the activation energy.
2 Iodine molecules are involved in the rate determining step.
3 The reaction is autocatalytic.
4 The reaction has an overall order of 2.

23 Which of the following properties is/are NOT shown by ANY of the elements carbon, silicon, tin and lead?

1 Forming an amphoteric oxide.
2 Existing in more than one oxidation state.
3 Forming a chloride which is hydrolysed by water.
4 Forming a hydride which gives an acidic aqueous solution.

24 Which of the following, with suitable measurements, would enable a determination to be made of the volume of 4 M sodium hydroxide solution required for neutralization of a solution of approximately 4 M hydrochloric acid contaminated by a blue dyestuff?

1 Thermometer.
2 pH meter.
3 Conductivity meter.
4 Litmus solution.

25 Chromium forms the complex ion $[Cr(NH_3)_6]^{3+}$. Which of the following statements would you expect to be true?

1 The correct name is the hexamminechromium(III) ion.
2 The complex ion is colourless.
3 The complex ion is octahedral.
4 A solution of the ions gives an immediate precipitate of chromium(III) hydroxide on addition of cold aqueous sodium hydroxide.

26 1 M solutions of copper(II) sulphate and ammonium sulphate were mixed in the volume ratio 1:2, giving a light blue solution.

Which of the following aqueous reagents, added to the mixture in slight excess, would give a deep blue solution?

1 Copper(II) sulphate.
2 Sodium hydroxide.
3 Ammonium sulphate.
4 Ammonia.

27 A mixture of unsaturated hydrocarbons containing double bonds would be expected to:

1 react with alkaline potassium manganate(VII) (potassium permanganate) solution.
2 decolorize a solution of bromine in hexane.
3 be soluble in ice-cold concentrated sulphuric acid.

4 be nitrated by a mixture of concentrated nitric and sulphuric acids.

Section III

Questions 28–32

Directions Each of the questions or incomplete statements in this section is followed by five suggested answers. Select the best answer in each case.

28 An organic compound can be characterized by the preparation of a crystalline derivative. The derivative *must*:

A have a higher solubility than the original compound in the solvent used.
B have a sharp melting point.
C decompose at its melting point.
D have a low relative molecular mass.
E have a sharp boiling point.

29 How many moles of zinc manganate(VII) [$Zn(MnO_4)_2$] are needed to react completely with 30 cm^3 of acidified 0.1 M iron(II) sulphate solution?

$$MnO_4^- + 8H^+ + 5e^- \rightarrow Mn^{2+} + 4H_2O$$

$$Fe^{2+} \rightarrow Fe^{3+} + e^-$$

A 3×10^{-2} B 7.5×10^{-3} C 1.2×10^{-3}
D 6×10^{-4} E 3×10^{-4}

30 Archaeologists can determine the age of organic matter by measuring the proportion of $^{14}_{6}C$ present. Assuming that carbon-14 has a half-life of 5600 years, a piece of wood found to contain $\frac{1}{8}$ as much carbon-14 as living material is calculated to have an age, in years, of:

A 44 800 B 16 800 C 2800 D 1400 E 700

31 The standard enthalpies of combustion of carbon,

hydrogen and methane are −394, −286 and −891 kJ mol^{-1}, respectively. Which one of the following expressions gives the correct value for the enthalpy of formation of methane?

A $394+(2\times 286)-891$ B $-394-(2\times 286)+891$
C $394+286-891$ D $-394-286+891$
E $-394-(4\times 286)+891$

32 Which combination of reagents should be used in order to obtain the final product in the reaction shown below?

$R.CH_2Br \rightarrow R.CH_2.CN \rightarrow R.CH_2.COOH$

A Aqueous potassium cyanide (KCN) followed by lithium tetrahydridoaluminate(III) (lithium aluminium hydride, $LiAlH_4$).
B Alcoholic potassium cyanide (KCN) followed by reflux with dilute acid.
C Alcoholic potassium cyanide (KCN) followed by lithium tetrahydridoaluminate(III) (lithium aluminium hydride, $LiAlH_4$).
D Alcoholic potassium cyanide (KCN) followed by reflux with acidified potassium manganate(VII) (potassium permanganate).
E Alcoholic potassium cyanide (KCN) followed by hydrogen in the presence of a nickel catalyst.

Questions 33–34

Directions Each of the questions or incomplete statements in this section is followed by five suggested answers. Select the best answer in each case.

33 Treatment of $CH_3CHBrCH_3$ with solid sodium methoxide (CH_3ONa) would give:

A $CH_3.CH(ONa).CH_3$ B $CH_3.CH(OH).CH_3$
C $CH_3.CH(OCH_3).CH_3$ D $CH_3.CH{=}CH_2$
E $CH_3.CH(CH_3)_2$

34 What is the pH of the buffer solution formed by mixing equal volumes of solutions of 0.1 M propanoic acid and 0.1 M sodium propanoate? (The dissociation constant for propanoic acid = 1.3×10^{-5} mol ℓ.)

A 1.00 B 1.30 C 3.11 D 4.89 E 5.11

Section IV

Questions 35–41

Directions Each of the following questions consists of a statement in the left-hand column followed by a second statement in the right-hand column.

Decide whether the first statement is true or false.
Decide whether the second statement is true or false.

Then on the answer sheet mark:

A if both statements are true and the second statement is a correct explanation of the first statement.
B if both statements are true but the second statement is NOT a correct explanation of the first statement.
C if the first statement is true but the second statement is false.
D if the first statement is false, but the second statement is true.
E if both statements are false.

Directions summarized

Answer	First Statement	Second Statement	
A	True	True	Second statement is a correct explanation of the first.
B	True	True	Second statement is NOT a correct explanation of the first.
C	True	False	
D	False	True	
E	False	False	

	First statement	Second statement
35	The bromine molecule is more polar than the iodine molecule.	The bromine atom has a larger electron affinity than the iodine atom.
36	Phenol is more acidic than ethanol.	The benzene ring in phenol withdraws electrons from the —OH group, whereas the ethyl group in ethanol does not.
37	For the series NaCl, NaBr and NaI, the change $NaX(s) \rightarrow Na^+(g) + X^-(g)$ becomes less endothermic.	Ionic radius decreases in the order Cl^-, Br^-, I^-.
38	The boron trifluoride molecule is planar, with a F—B—F bond angle of 120°.	The boron trifluoride molecule has three bond pairs of electrons with no lone pair of electrons on the boron atom.
39	Ethanoic acid does NOT give a precipitate with 2,4-dinitrophenylhydrazine reagent.	The —OH group in ethanoic acid modifies the properties of the adjacent >C=O group.
40	A catalyst can alter the composition of an equilibrium mixture.	A catalyst will affect the rates of the forward and reverse reactions to a different extent.
41	The boiling point of propan-1-ol is higher than that of ethanol.	Hydrogen bonding occurs in propan-1-ol, but not in ethanol.

Section V

Questions 42–50

Directions This group of questions deals with laboratory situations. Each situation is followed by a set of questions.

Select the best answer for each question.

Questions 42–45 concern an experiment to find the enthalpy of hydration of anhydrous copper(II) sulphate in which the enthalpies of solution of anhydrous copper(II) sulphate and copper(II) sulphate crystals ($CuSO_4 . 5H_2O$) were determined.

The following procedure was carried out with each solid separately.

0.025 moles of the solid were weighed out. The temperature of a known mass of water in a polystyrene [poly(phenylethene)] cup was measured and the solid was added to the water. The mixture was stirred continuously with the thermometer and the temperature noted frequently until a steady value was obtained.

42 The most important reason for using a polystyrene [poly(phenylethene)] cup for a calorimeter rather than a glass vessel is that:

A accidental breakage of the calorimeter is avoided should it be knocked over.
B the calorimeter would not crack if a sharp rise in temperature occurred when the solid was added to the water.
C the cup is cheap and can be thrown away after use.
D the thermal capacity of the cup is small.
E the bulb of the thermometer will not be damaged during stirring.

43 The temperature rise was 8.0°C, measured to an accuracy of 0.1°C, when 4 g of anhydrous copper(II) sulphate was dissolved in 50.0 g of water. The copper(II) sulphate should be weighed to an accuracy of at least:

A 1 g B 0.5 g C 0.05 g D 0.005 g E 0.0005 g

44 The temperature rise which occurred when the anhydrous salt was dissolved in 50 g of water was lower than data book figures suggested. This could have been caused by all of the following EXCEPT:

A some of the solid remaining undissolved.
B accidentally weighed out more than 4 g of salt.
C the calorimeter standing in a cooling draught.
D the salt being partly hydrated.
E accidentally using more than 50 g of water.

45. The standard of enthalpies of solution of the anhydrous salt and the hydrated salt are -66.1 and $+11.3\,\text{kJ mol}^{-1}$, respectively. The standard enthalpy of the hydration of anhydrous copper(II) sulphate, in kJ mol^{-1}, is:

A -77.4 B -54.8 C $+54.8$
D $+77.4$ E Impossible to determine from these data.

Questions 46–50 concern an experiment in which the apparatus in Figure 1 was used to compare the rates of effusion of various gases through a small aperture under the mass of the piston at constant temperature.

For two gases

$$\frac{t_1}{t_2} = \sqrt{\frac{M_1}{M_2}}$$

where t is the time taken for a fixed volume of gas of relative molecular mass, M, to effuse.

$75\,\text{cm}^3$ of butane, C_4H_{10}, take 20 s to effuse.

(Relative atomic masses: H = 1; C = 12; N = 14; O = 16; S = 32; Cl = 35.5; Kr = 84).

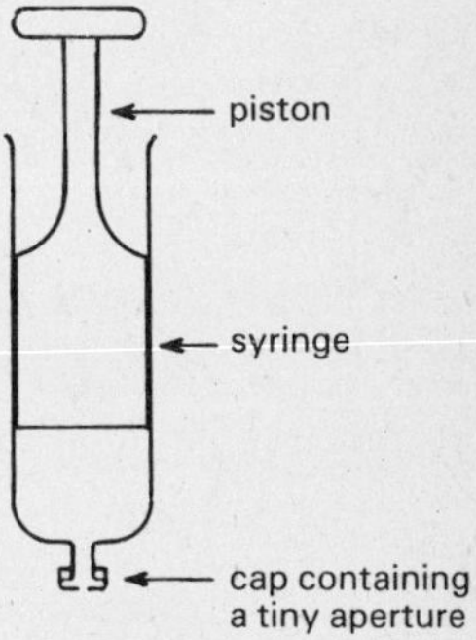

Figure 1

46 $75\,\text{cm}^3$ of hydrogen, at the same temperature and atmospheric pressure would be expected to take approximately:

A 0.5 s B 1.2 s C 2.5 s D 3.7 s E 6.1 s

47 Another pure gas was tested under the same conditions as the butane and hydrogen. It took approximately 14 s for 75 cm^3 to effuse. The gas could have been:

A carbon dioxide. B sulphur dioxide.
C chlorine. D krypton.
E nitrogen.

48 A knowledge of the kinetic theory of gases suggests that the factor most likely to be responsible for gases having different effusion times at constant temperature is the difference in their:

A internal molecular vibrations.
B average molecular spacing.
C average molecular size.
D average molecular velocity.
E average molecular kinetic energy.

49 The gases were well dried before being led into the syringe. This was necessary because of the possible effect of water vapour in changing the sample's:

A chemical structure. B density. C buoyancy.
D temperature. E tendency to condense in the aperture

50 It is most important that the previous gas, *X*, is removed completely before filling the syringe with the sample of the next gas to be tested *Y*. The best way to accomplish this would be to:

A expel *X* by pushing the piston home once only.
B flush with air, then push the piston home.
C dismantle, wash, and dry the syringe.
D flush the syringe several times with gas *Y*.
E evacuate the syringe, using a laboratory water pump.

(All L)

Answers and comments

1 E Naphthalene is a covalent molecular solid.

2 C Carbon monoxide is a covalently bonded gas.

3 B Graphite, a solid allotrope of carbon, has a macromolecular lattice.

4 B Silicon(IV) oxide consists of a lattice made up of covalently bonded SiO_4 units.

5 D Helium, a noble gas, has monatomic molecules.

6 A Caesium chloride is ionic, being the compound of a reactive metal and a non metal.

7 E Carbon monoxide is one of the products of the dehydration of ethandioic acid.

8 A Ethan-1,2-diol can be oxidized to ethandioic acid as it contains two primary alcohol groups.

9 C Phenol is a weaker acid than carbonic acid. It therefore reacts with strong alkalis, but does not displace carbon dioxide from carbonates.

10 C Formation of esters is a characteristic of compounds containing the hydroxyl (—OH) group. Alcohols form esters when treated both with acid chlorides and acids. Phenols, with the —OH attached to an aromatic (benzene) nucleus, only do so with acid chlorides.

11 D Formation of tri-iodomethane is indicative of the presence of a $CH_3-\overset{|}{\underset{\underset{H}{|}}{C}}-OH$ group, present only in D.

12 B As normal chemical methods are not stereospecific, the compound must be prepared as a mixture of two optical (stereo) isomers and hence contains an asymmetrically substituted carbon atom.

13 C Hydrogen, one of the elements required to synthesize ammonia, is obtained in quantity from natural gas, methane being the major constituent of this.

14 A This reaction indicates the presence of a $-C{\equiv}C-H$ group, present only in ethyne.

15 E A, B and C are gases at 20°C. D reacts with hydrogen with a nickel catalyst. E is the only saturated liquid.

16 B This reaction removes water from ethanol, giving ethene.

17 D Of the two liquids, D and E, E only reacts with chlorine to give substitution products whereas D can react both by substitution and addition.

18 B 6 ℓ is $\frac{1}{4}$ mole. As 4 g is $\frac{1}{8}$ mole oxygen and 20 g is $\frac{1}{2}$ mole argon, 2 and 4 are incorrect.

19 A Ethanoic acid may be reduced (1), contains an —OH group therefore reacts with PCl_5 (2) and reacts with carbonates (3). It is not oxidized by manganate(VII).

20 E Coloured ions have an incompletely filled *d* orbital. 1, 3 and 4 either have no *d* orbital or have a completely filled *d* orbital, hence these are all colourless.

21 A 4 is incorrect as magnesium sulphate is soluble.

22 B If a substance catalyses a reaction it does so because it reduces the activation energy. As hydrogen ions are produced in the reaction, it is autocatalytic. Hence 1 and 3 are correct. If a reaction is zero order with respect to a reactant, that substance is not involved in the rate-determining step; hence 2 is incorrect. Overall order of reaction can only be determined by experiment, and depends on the number of molecules involved in the rate-determining step. The information given is insufficient to deduce the overall order in this case; hence 4 is incorrect.

23 D One or more of the named elements have a property listed in 1, 2 and 3. None of the named elements is sufficiently electronegative to form a polar hydride which would give an acidic aqueous solution.

24 A The reaction of the named reagents would
(i) be exothermic.
(ii) involve a change of pH.
(iii) also involve a change of conductivity.
Hence, 1, 2 and 3 are correct. The presence of a blue dyestuff would mean that the colour change of the indicator would be obscured.

25 B 2 is incorrect as this is a transition metal complex—all chromium-containing compounds are coloured. 4 is incorrect as the properties of a complex ion are different from those of its constituents.

26 D Only 4 is correct, as the deep blue complex is given when a solution containing copper ions is reacted with an excess of aqueous ammonia.

27 A 1, 2 and 3 are reactions of organic compounds containing double bonds. 4 is a reaction of an aromatic compound.

28 B The melting point of a readily prepared and separated crystalline derivative of an organic compound is specific to a particular substance and hence may be used to characterize that substance.

29 E 1 mole MnO_4^- is equivalent to 5 moles Fe^{2+}. 30 cm^3 0.1 M Fe^{2+} contains $\frac{30 \times 0.1}{1000}$ moles Fe^{2+} and hence requires $\frac{1}{5} \times 3 \times 10^{-3}$ moles MnO_4^-. As zinc manganate(VII) contains 2 moles MnO_4^- per mole, number of moles of this required $= \frac{1}{2} \times \frac{1}{5} \times 3 \times 10^{-3}$ moles $= 3 \times 10^{-4}$ moles.

30 B $\frac{1}{8} = (\frac{1}{2})^3$. Hence the material has an age of 3 half-lives $= 3 \times 5600$ years $= 16\,800$ years.

31 B $\Delta H_f = \Delta H_{comb}C + 2 \times \Delta H_{comb}H_2 - \Delta H_{comb}CH_4$

$$= -394 + 2(-286) - (-894)\ \text{kJ mol}^{-1}.$$

32 B Reaction with alcoholic KCN replaces halogen by the nitrile group. Acids may be obtained by acid hydrolysis of nitriles.

33 C These substances would react by nucleophilic substitution of Br^- by CH_3O^-.

34 D pH of a buffer $= -\log_{10} K_a + \log_{10} \frac{[\text{salt}]}{[\text{acid}]}$

as $[\text{salt}] = [\text{acid}]\ \log_{10} \frac{[\text{salt}]}{[\text{acid}]} = 0.$

Hence, in this case $\text{pH} = -\log_{10} K_a$. As $K_a = 1.3 \times 10^{-5}$, $-\log_{10} K_a$ will be slightly less than 5.

35 D The first statement is incorrect, as polarity only occurs when two atoms with different electronegatives are bonded together. Statement 2 is correct as the electron is being gained, in bromine, by an orbital closer to the nucleus than in iodine.

36 A Both statements are correct. Phenol dissolves in aqueous sodium hydroxide, whereas alcohol does not react. The second statement explains the first, as withdrawal of electrons from the oxygen results in weakening of the O—H bond.

37 C The change becomes less endothermic as the halogens have different electronegatives. The second statement is incorrect as iodine has the largest atomic radius and hence largest ionic radius.

38 A Both statements are correct. BF_3 is an sp^2 hybrid, the three bonding pairs being at a maximum distance apart results in the quoted bond angle.

39 A Reaction with 2,4-dinitrophenylhydrazine is a characteristic of the >C=O group and as stated the properties of that group are modified in the acid by the presence of the —OH group on the same carbon atom.

40 E A catalyst lowers the energy barrier to the same extent for both forward and backward reactions, hence a catalyst affects the rate of both forward and backward reactions to the same extent. The use of a catalyst does not, therefore, alter the composition of an equilibrium mixture.

41 C Propan-1-ol has an extra $—CH_2—$ unit to ethanol. Hydrogen bonding occurs in both molecules. The difference in bp is because of the extra numbers of electrons associated with the $—CH_2—$ unit increasing the strength of the Van der Waals attraction which contributes to the attraction between the molecules.

42 D Plastics, particularly expanded polystyrene [poly(phenylethene)], generally have low thermal capacities. This results in heat losses from the solutions to the calorimeter being low. The other reasons quoted relate to handling problems, and would not affect the accuracy of the result.

43 C The accuracy of measurement of the temperature change is 0.1 parts in 8 (ie, 1 part in 80). The weighing should be to at least this degree of accuracy, if not better. B gives an error of 0.5 in 4 (ie, 1 in 8), C an error of 0.05 parts in 4 (ie, 1 in 80), D of 1 in 800—hence C is the correct response.

44 B If more copper salt were weighed, then an increased temperature change would be obtained resulting in a higher value than expected. The other causes would all result in a lower value.

45 A The enthalpy change is, numerically, the difference between the two values. As the temperature increased in the experiment, then the reaction must be exothermic, hence the sign is negative.

46 D Substituting $t_2=20$, $M_1=2$, $M_2=58$, then $t_1 = \frac{\sqrt{2}}{\sqrt{58}} \times 20$ which is less than $(\frac{1}{5} \times 20)$ s.

47 E Substituting $t_1=14$, $t_2=20$, $M_2=58$. $\sqrt{M_1}=\frac{14}{20}\sqrt{58}$ $M_1 \sim \frac{1}{2} \times 58 \sim 29$. The only gas with Mr approximately this value is nitrogen $(2 \times 14=28)$.

48 D For a gas to effuse more rapidly than another, its molecules must be moving more rapidly.

49 B As Mr $\sim 2 \times$ density, the presence of water vapour would affect the density and hence the value for Mr, giving a changed rate of effusion.

50 D A would result in some of X remaining in the syringe. B in some air remaining. C in some air and possibly water remaining. E also in some air remaining as a laboratory water pump does not give a complete vacuum.

Chapter 2

Atomic and molecular mass determination

Example 1

(a) Explain briefly how a knowledge of the density of a gaseous compound leads to a value for its relative molecular mass, independent of its chemical composition.

(b) Find the relative molecular mass of a liquid, 0.15 g of which on vaporization gives 30 cm^3 of vapour measured at 373K and a pressure of 1 atm (ie, 10^2 kN m^{-2}). The gas constant is 0.0821 ℓ atm K^{-1} mol^{-1} or 8.31 JK^{-1} mol^{-1}.

(c) When the values obtained for the relative molecular masses from gas densities are compared with those obtained from the chemical formulae and accurate relative masses, it may be found that:

(i) The two values are approximately but not exactly the same; or

(ii) the gas density value is considerably less than the value found from the formula; or

(iii) the gas density value is approximately twice the value from the formula.

Discuss the reasons for these three types of discrepancy, giving examples.

(L)

Answer

(a) At STP one mole of all gases occupies 22.4 ℓ irrespective of chemical composition. From the density of a gas can be found the mass of 22.4 ℓ and hence the mass of one mole.

(b) $PV = nRT$, where n = number of moles and $R = 8.31\ \text{Jk}^{-1}\ \text{mol}^{-1}$

$$n = \frac{PV}{RT}$$

$$n = \frac{10^5 \times 30 \times 10^{-6}}{8.31 \times 373}$$

$n = 9.68 \times 10^{-4}$ moles

$\therefore$ 0.15 g of liquid represents 9.68×10^{-4} moles

$$\therefore \text{mass of one mole} = \frac{0.15}{9.68 \times 10^{-4}} = 155\ \text{g}$$

Relative molecular mass of the liquid is 155.

(c) (i) A slight discrepancy may be the result of experimental error or the non-ideal behaviour of the vapour. An example is the measurement of the relative molecular mass of trichloromethane by Dumas' method.

(ii) If the gas density value is too low it is an indication that thermal dissociation is taking place. For example ammonium chloride vapour dissociates on heating:

$$NH_4Cl \rightleftharpoons NH_3 + HCl$$

One volume of ammonium chloride produces two volumes of ammonia and hydrogen chloride on complete dissociation, and so the gas density would be halved.

(iii) If the gas density value is approximately doubled it is an indication that the molecules are undergoing association. For example, in the vapour state, aluminium chloride dimerizes:

$$2AlCl_3 \rightleftharpoons Al_2Cl_6$$

Thus for a given mass of vapour the volume will be halved.

Example 2

(a) Explain the terms *mass number* and *atomic number*.

4 *marks*

(b) (i) Describe briefly the principle of the mass spectrometer for measuring mass number.

(ii) Figure 2 is a mass spectrometer trace for a compound.

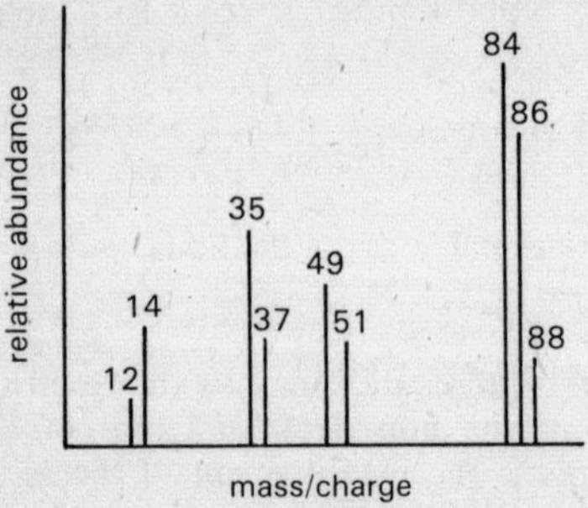

Figure 2

Suggest a value for the relative molecular mass of the compound and indicate two elements which it might contain.

7 *marks*

(c) Some properties of elements are a periodic function of their atomic numbers. Illustrate this statement by sketching the approximate relationship between a named property (NOT the ionization energy) and the atomic number for the elements from hydrogen to potassium.

3 *marks*

(L)

Answer

(a) The mass number is the total number of neutrons and protons in one atom of an element.

The atomic number is the number of protons in one atom of an element.

(b) **(i)** A beam of ions is deflected by a magnetic field perpendicular to its path. The deflection for ions of the same charge travelling at the same speed is inversely proportional to the square root of their masses. After passing through the magnetic field, the ions fall on to a photographic plate and produce a mass spectrum, which is a series of lines. The relative masses of the particles can be deduced from the positions of the lines.

(ii) The relative molecular mass lies between 84 and 88. The compound may contain carbon (Ar = 12) or chlorine (Ar = 35 or 37).

(c) See Figure 3 for one example. Other properties that can be used include:

melting point.
atomic radius.

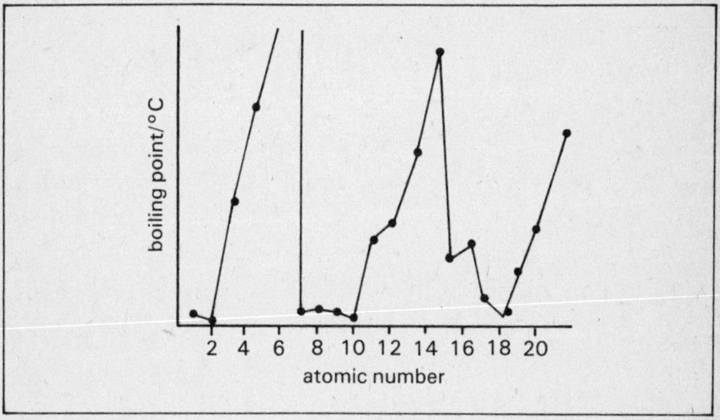

Figure 3

Example 3

(a) Explain what is meant by each of the following terms:
(i) electron. (ii) proton. (iii) neutron. (iv) isotopes.

2 marks

(b) The atomic number provides three pieces of information about an element. What are they?

3 marks

(c) The radioactive atom $^{224}_{88}Ra$ decays by α-emission with a half-life of 3.64 days.

(i) What is meant by 'half-life' of 3.64 days?

(ii) Referring to the products of the decay, what will be its mass number, its atomic number?

(iii) Radium is in Group II of the Periodic Table. In what Group will the decay product be?

4 marks

(d) Explain briefly the principles underlying:

(i) the use of radioactive isotopes as 'tracers'.

(ii) the dating of dead organic matter using radiocarbon, $^{14}_{6}C$.

6 marks

(L)

Answer

(a) **(i)** A particle or wave carrying one unit of negative charge.

(ii) A particle in the nucleus of one atomic mass unit and carrying one unit of positive charge.

(iii) A particle in the nucleus of one atomic mass unit and zero charge.

(iv) Elements having the same atomic number but different mass numbers.

(b) **(i)** The number of protons.

(ii) The number of electrons in the neutral atom.

(iii) The position in the periodic table.

(c) **(i)** The time taken for half the initial amount of radium atoms to decay is 3.64 days.

(ii) Mass number 220, atomic number 86.

(iii) Group 0.

(d) (i) A radioactive isotope of an element may be introduced to a strategic position in a compound. After a series of reactions investigation of the position of the isotope in the products can give information about the pathways and mechanism.

(ii) Living matter incorporates carbon from atmospheric carbon dioxide. The ratio $^{14}CO_2$ to $^{12}CO_2$ is almost constant, and so the ratio ^{14}C to ^{12}C in the living plant is constant. After death the ^{14}C decays, and the age may be determined from the new ratio.

Example 4

(a) (i) Define the terms *mass number* and *atomic number.* 2 *marks*

(ii) The mass spectrum of the element boron is shown in Figure 4.

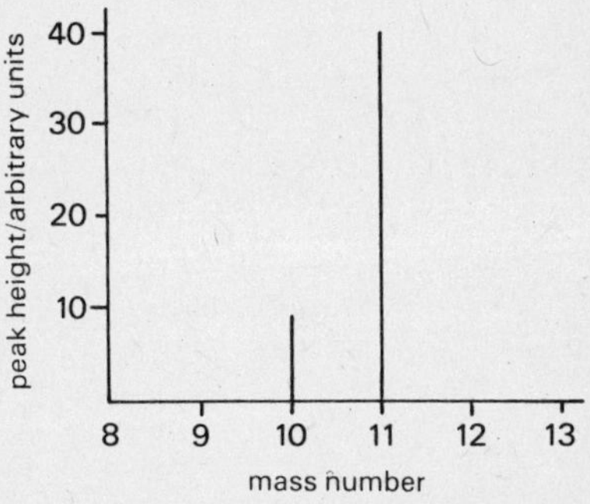

Figure 4

Calculate the relative atomic mass of the element boron. 3 *marks*

(AEB part qu: Nov 1978)

Answer

(a) (i) See Example 2 p. 26.

(ii) From the graph there are 9 parts ^{10}B to 40 parts ^{11}B.

$$\text{Relative atomic mass} = \frac{9}{49} \times 10 + \frac{40}{49} \times 11$$

$$= 10.8$$

Chapter 3
Physical and chemical equilibria

Example 1

This question is about the reversible reaction:

$$2HI(g) \rightleftharpoons H_2(g) + I_2(g)$$

(a) Using this system as an example, explain what is meant by

(i) equilibrium mixture.
(ii) equilibrium constant, K_c.

It can be shown that if some radioactive iodine is added to the equilibrium mixture, the iodine in the hydrogen iodide also becomes radioactive. What can be deduced from this observation? 4 *marks*

(b) In an experiment to determine K_c, 0.210 g of hydrogen iodide was heated at 800K in a bulb of volume 100 cm^3 until equilibrium was attained. The bulb was broken under potassium iodide solution and the iodine present found to be sufficient to react with 4.0 cm^3 of sodium thiosulphate solution, concentration 0.1 mol ℓ^{-1}.

$(2S_2O_3{}^{2-} + I_2 = 2I^- + S_4O_6{}^{2-})$

(i) Why was it adequate to absorb the iodine at room temperature although its amount at the high temperature of the experiment was actually required?

(ii) Calculate:

The number of moles of hydrogen iodide in 0.210 g.

The number of moles of iodine (I_2) formed in the experiment.

Hence find:

The number of moles of hydrogen (H_2) also formed.

The number of moles of hydrogen iodide left unreacted.

(iii) Calculate K_c for the reaction at 800K. 7 *marks*

(c) The bulb had a volume of $100\,cm^3$. If a $200\,cm^3$ bulb had been used, what values would have been obtained for the following?

(i) The number of moles of iodine present at equilibrium.

(ii) The equilibrium constant.

Explain your answer. 3 *marks*

(L)

Answer

(a) **(i)** The mixture of hydrogen iodide, hydrogen and iodine present when the reaction has reached equilibrium, ie, constant concentrations of reactants and products.

(ii) $$K_c = \frac{[H_2(g)]eq\,[I_2(g)]eq}{[HI(g)]^2\,eq}$$

Both forward and reverse reactions continue at equilibrium.

(b) **(i)** Although the equilibrium position has altered, the rate of reaction at room temperature is very slow.

(ii) $Mr(HI) = 1 + 127 = 128$

$$\text{Amount of HI} = \frac{0.210}{123} = 1.64 \times 10^{-3}\,\text{mol}$$

$$\text{Amount of sodium thiosulphate} = \frac{4 \times 0.1}{1000}\,\text{mol}$$

One mole of iodine reacts with two moles of thiosulphate:

$$\therefore \text{Amount of iodine} = \frac{4 \times 0.1}{2 \times 1000} = 2 \times 10^{-4}\,\text{mol}$$

For each mole of iodine one mole of hydrogen is formed:

$\therefore$ amount of hydrogen $= 2 \times 10^{-4}$ mol

For each mole of iodine and hydrogen formed, two

moles of hydrogen iodide react:

$\therefore$ amount of HI unreacted $= 1.64 \times 10^{-3} - 4 \times 10^{-4}$
$= 1.24 \times 10^{-3}$ mol

(iii) $K_c = \dfrac{2 \times 10^{-4} \times 2 \times 10^{-4}}{(1.24 \times 10^{-3})^2}$

$= 0.026$

(c) (i) 2×10^{-4} mol
(ii) $K_c = 0.026$

The equilibrium is unaffected by a change in pressure (caused by a change in volume of the bulb) since there are equal numbers of molecules on each side of the equation. K_c only changes with changes in temperature.

Example 2

(a) For the reaction $2SO_2(g) + O_2(g) \rightleftharpoons 2SO_3(g)$, write an expression for the equilibrium K_p and K_c. *4 marks*

(b) When 2 moles of sulphur dioxide and 1 mole of oxygen are reacted at 750K and a pressure of 10^5Pa (1 atm approximately) in the presence of a catalyst, three-quarters of the sulphur dioxide is converted into sulphur(VI) oxide (sulphur trioxide).

(i) Calculate the equilibrium constant, K_p, of this reaction. *6 marks*

(ii) Name a suitable catalyst for this reaction and explain why a catalyst is necessary. *6 marks*

(c) The enthalpy change of the forward reaction in (a) is negative. Explain, qualitatively, how the equilibrium partial pressure of sulphur trioxide, SO_3, will be altered by:

(i) halving the volume of the system at constant temperature. *3 marks*

(ii) adding sulphur dioxide, SO_2, at constant volume and constant temperature. *3 marks*

(iii) lowering the temperature while keeping the volume constant. *3 marks*

(AEB: Nov 1978)

Answer

(a) $K_p = \dfrac{P(SO_3)^2}{P(SO_2)^2 \times P(O_2)}$

where $P(SO_3)$, etc, refer to equilibrium partial pressures.

$$K_c = \frac{[SO_3(g)]^2\,eq}{[SO_2(g)]^2\,eq\,[O_2(g)]\,eq}$$

(b) (i) $2SO_2 + O_2 \rightleftharpoons 2SO_3$

$2SO_2$	O_2	$2SO_3$	
2	1	0	initial amount (mol)
0.5	0.25	1.5	equilib. amount (mol)

Total amount at equilibrium = 2.25 mol

$\frac{0.5}{2.25}$	$\frac{0.25}{2.25}$	$\frac{1.5}{2.25}$	mole fraction
$\frac{2}{9} \times 10^5$	$\frac{1}{9} \times 10^5$	$\frac{2}{3} \times 10^5$	partial pressure (Pa)

$$K_p = \frac{\left(\frac{2}{3} \times 10^5\right)^2}{\left(\frac{2}{9} \times 10^5\right)^2 \left(\frac{1}{9} \times 10^5\right)}$$

$$= 8.1 \times 10^{-4}\ Pa^{-1}$$

(ii) Vanadium(V) oxide. The reaction would proceed too slowly without a catalyst and take a long time to reach equilibrium.

(c) (i) Halving the volume increases the pressure and, by Le Chatelier's principle, will force the equilibrium towards the product side. The partial pressure of SO_3 will increase.

(ii) Adding SO_2 will increase $P(SO_2)$. This will cause $P(SO_3)$ to increase and $P(O_2)$ to decrease, as K_p must remain constant.

(iii) Since the enthalpy change for the forward reaction is negative, heat is given out during the reaction. Lowering the temperature will, by Le Chatelier's principle, encourage formation of products. $P(SO_3)$ will increase.

Example 3

(a) State carefully Raoult's law of vapour pressure lowering.

4 *marks*

(b) A 4.0% solution of ribitol in water (ie, 4 g in 100 g of solution) has the same boiling point as a 4.5% solution of glucose ($C_6H_{12}O_6 = 180$) in water. Calculate the molar mass of ribitol.

4 *marks*

(c) If the apparent degree of ionization of potassium chloride (KCl = 74.5) in water at 290K is 0.86, calculate the mass of potassium chloride that must be made up to 1 dm³ (1 ℓ) of aqueous solution to have the same osmotic pressure as the solution of glucose at that temperature.

4 *marks*

(SUJB part qu.)

Answer

(a) Raoult's law.
The relative lowering of vapour pressure of a solution is equal to the mole fraction of solute. This holds for dilute solutions of involatile solutes that do not dissociate nor react with the solvent.

(b) As the two solutions have the same boiling point, the mole fractions of ribitol and glucose must be equal.

$$\therefore \left(\frac{m}{\text{Mr}}\right)_{\text{glucose}} = \left(\frac{m}{\text{Mr}}\right)_{\text{ribitol}}$$

where m is the mass of solute in 100 g of water and Mr is the relative molecular mass.

$$\therefore \frac{4.5}{180} = \frac{4}{Mr}$$

$\therefore$ Mr(ribitol) = 160

(c) Solutions of the same molar concentration at the same temperature produce the same osmotic pressure.

$$\text{Concentration of glucose} = \frac{45}{180} \text{ mol } \ell^{-1}$$

KCl ionizes in solution to produce 1.86 moles of particles per mole of KCl.

$$\therefore \text{ concentration of KCl required} = \frac{45}{180 \times 1.86} \text{ mol } \ell^{-1}$$

$$\therefore \text{ mass of KCl required per } \ell = \frac{45 \times 74.5}{180 \times 1.86} \text{ g}$$

$$= 10 \text{ g}$$

Example 4

The graph shown in Figure 5 represents the partial vapour pressures of the miscible liquids dioxane and water above various mixtures of the two liquids at 35°C.

The structure of dioxane is:

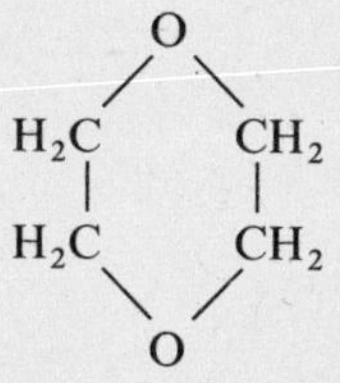

(a) (i) Using the values on the graph, plot accurately, on the same axes, a line that would correspond to the variation of total vapour pressure with composition for any mixture of the two liquids. Label this line 'Line A'.

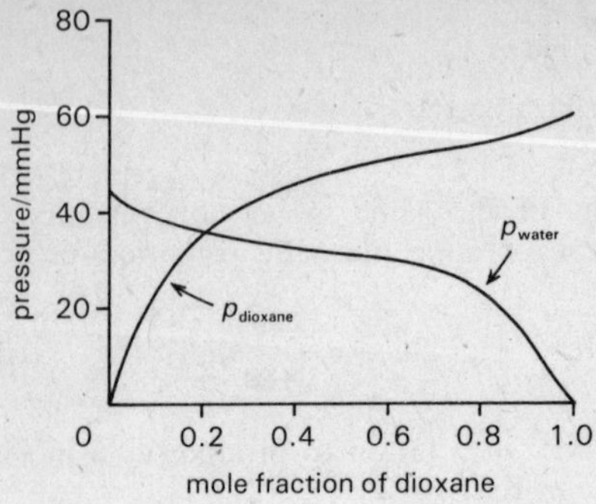

Figure 5

(ii) Also on the same axes, draw accurately a line to represent the variation of total vapour pressure with composition for any mixture of the two liquids, had the liquids behaved ideally and obeyed Raoult's Law. Label this line 'Line B'.

3 *marks*

(b) What would be the actual vapour pressure of water over a mixture containing a mole fraction of 0.8 of water and 0.2 of dioxane?

1 *mark*

(c) What would be the actual total vapour pressure over a mixture containing 9 g of water and 132 g of dioxane? (Relative atomic masses: H = 1; C = 12; O = 16.)

3 *marks*

(d) What type of interaction predominates between molecules in:

(i) pure water?

(ii) pure dioxane? 2 *marks*

(e) Explain, in terms of intermolecular forces, the deviation from Raoult's law that occurs in a mixture of water and dioxane.

3 *marks*
(NUFF)

Answer

(a) (i) and (ii). See Figure 6.

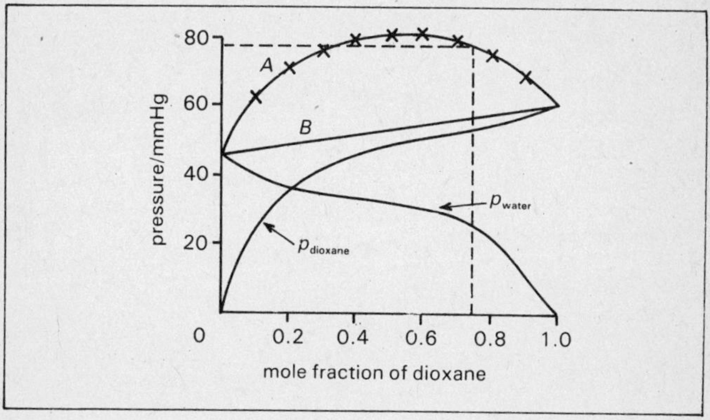

Figure 6

(b) 36 mm Hg (see Figure 6).

(c) Mr(dioxane) = 88, Mr(water) = 18.

$$\text{Amount of dioxane} = \frac{132}{88} = 1.5 \text{ mol}$$

$$\text{Amount of water} = \frac{9}{18} = 0.5 \text{ mol}$$

$$\text{Mole fraction dioxane} = \frac{1.5}{1.5 + 0.5} = 0.75 \text{ mol}$$

∴ Total vapour pressure = 79 mm Hg (from Figure 6).

(d) (i) Hydrogen bonds.
(ii) Van der Waals bonds.

(e) Water is extensively hydrogen bonded and dioxane is not. On mixing dioxane molecules cause water molecules to be separated. Some hydrogen bonds are broken to be replaced by weaker interactions. The molecules are less firmly held in the liquid phase, and the vapour pressure increases.

Example 5

(a) Heptane and octane form an *ideal* solution.

(i) Give a mathematical expression for Raoult's vapour pressure law for a solution of two liquids, A and B, explaining the terms used. 3 *marks*

(ii) Under what circumstances will a mixture of two liquids behave as an ideal solution? 2 *marks*

(iii) Calculate the vapour pressure of a solution containing 50 g heptane (C_7H_{16}) and 38 g octane (C_8H_{18}), at 20°C. [Ar(H)=1; Ar(C)=12]. The vapour pressure of heptane at 20°C=473.2 Pa. The vapour pressure of octane at 20°C =139.8 Pa. 6 *marks*

(b)

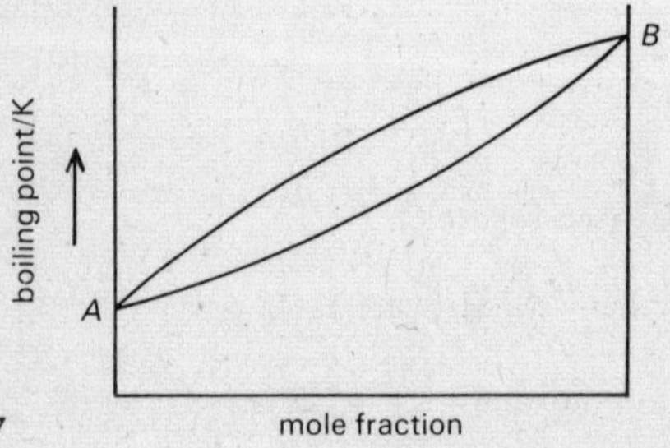

Figure 7

Figure 7 represents the boiling point/composition diagram for a solution of heptane and octane.

(i) What do the points A and B represent? 1 *mark*

(ii) An equimolar solution of heptane and octane is distilled. Mark on the diagram the temperature T at which the solution begins to boil and the point C giving the composition of the vapour given off when the solution begins to boil. 2 *marks*

(iii) Explain *briefly* how the solution can be separated into pure heptane and pure octane. 2 *marks*

(AEB: June 1979)

Answer

(a) (i) $P = X_A P_A^0 + X_B P_B^0$

where P is the total pressure, X_A and X_B are mole fractions of A and B.

P_A^0, P_B^0 are the saturated vapour pressures of A and B.

(ii) An ideal mixture of liquids is one in which the intermolecular forces in both liquids are identical. The liquids must be very similar compounds.

(iii) Mr(heptane) = 100, Mr(octane) = 114.

$$\text{Amount of heptane} = \frac{50}{100} = \frac{1}{2}\text{ mol}$$

$$\text{Amount of octane} = \frac{38}{114} = \frac{1}{3}\text{ mol}$$

$$X(\text{heptane}) = \frac{3}{5} \qquad X(\text{octane}) = \frac{2}{5}$$

$$\therefore\ P = \frac{3}{5} \times 473.2 + \frac{2}{5} \times 139.8\text{ Pa}$$

$$= 339.8\text{ Pa}$$

(b) (i) A is the boiling point of heptane and B the boiling point of octane.

(ii) See Figure 8.

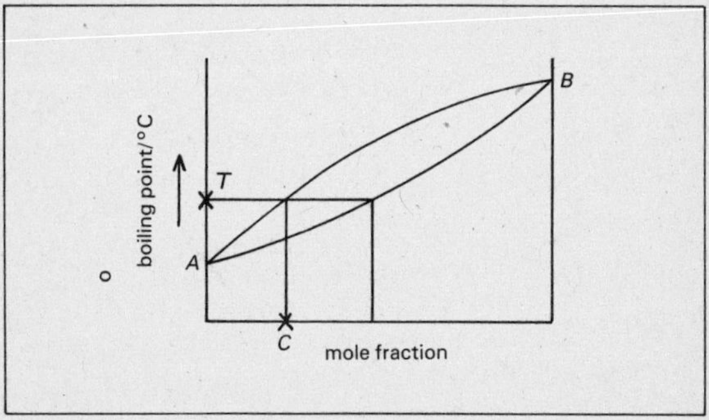

Figure 8

(iii) By fractional distillation. The mixture is boiled and the vapour passes up a vertical column packed with glass beads. At the top of the column pure heptane vapour passes into a condenser where it is collected as a liquid.

Example 6

Figure 9 shows the approximate vapour pressure/composition curve for liquid mixtures of water and propan-1-ol (which form non-ideal solutions) and the separate partial vapour pressures of water and propan-1-ol. Ideal behaviour is indicated by dotted lines.

Propan-1-ol and water form a constant boiling (azeotropic) mixture containing 0.43 mole fraction of propan-1-ol. This mixture boils at 88.1°C at 101.3 kPa (1 atm). At the same pressure water boils at 100°C and propan-1-ol at 97.2°C.

(a) In Figure 9 sketch the corresponding boiling point/composition curve for solutions of these two liquids showing how the vapour-composition curve differs from the liquid-composition curve.

4 *marks*

(b) With reference to Figure 9, explain what occurs when the following mixtures are distilled:

(i) a mixture containing 0.3 mole fraction of propan-1-ol.

3 *marks*

(ii) a mixture containing 0.8 mole fraction of propan-1-ol.

3 *marks*

(c) In the preparation of phenylamine (aniline) from nitrobenzene, the phenylamine is recovered from the reaction by *steam distillation.*

What is meant by *steam distillation*, and what are the properties of those compounds for which the process is suitable?

5 *marks*

(AEB: Nov 1978)

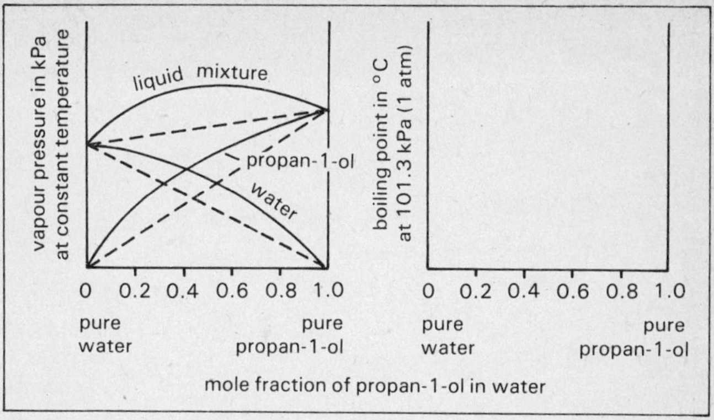

Figure 9

Answer

(a) See Figure 10.

(b) **(i)** The mixture will boil initially at a little over 88°C. The vapour becomes richer in propan-1-ol until the azeotropic mixture distils leaving pure water behind.

(ii) The azeotropic mixture will distil leaving pure propan-1-ol in the flask.

(c) Steam is passed through the heated mixture and phenylamine and water codistil. The phenylamine will distil at a temperature below 100°C. Properties: high boiling-point compounds that tend to decompose near their own boiling-point.

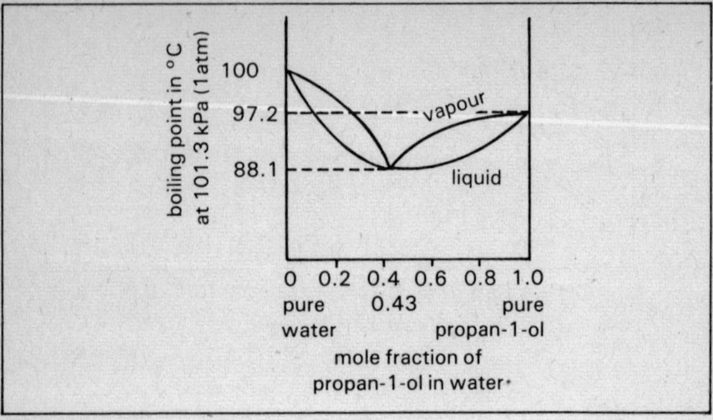
boiling point in °C
at 101.3 kPa (1 atm)
100
97.2
88.1
vapour
liquid
0
0.2
0.4
0.6
0.8
1.0
pure
water
0.43
pure
propan-1-ol
mole fraction of
propan-1-ol in water

Figure 10

Chapter 4
Thermodynamics and reaction kinetics

Example 1

(a) Define:

(i) standard enthalpy of formation.
(ii) standard enthalpy of combustion. *2 marks*

(b) The standard enthalpy changes, in $kJ\,mol^{-1}$, of the following reactions refer to a temperature of 298K:

$$C(s) + O_2(g) \rightarrow CO_2(g) \qquad \Delta H = -394$$

$$H_2(g) + \tfrac{1}{2}O_2(g) \rightarrow H_2O(l) \qquad \Delta H = -286$$

$$C_2H_4(g) + 3O_2(g) \rightarrow 2CO_2(g) + 2H_2O(l) \quad \Delta H = -1411$$

Calculate the standard enthalpy of formation of ethene.

4 marks

(c) If, at 298K, the enthalpy of sublimation is $713\,kJ\,mol^{-1}$ and the bond energy terms H—H and C—H are 436 and $415\,kJ\,mol^{-1}$, respectively, calculate the C=C bond energy term.

7 marks

(d) When ethene is burned in oxygen, does the entropy increase, decrease or stay the same? Explain your answer. Assume that the reactants and products are at 298K.

2 marks
(L)

Answer

(a) (i) The enthalpy change when one mole of a compound is formed from the elements under standard conditions (reactants and products at 298K, 1 atmosphere pressure).

(ii) The enthalpy change when one mole of a compound is completely burnt in excess oxygen under standard conditions.

(b)

	ΔH/kJ mol^{-1}
$2H_2(g) + O_2(g) \rightarrow 2H_2O(l)$	$2 \times (-286)$
$2C(s) + 2O_2(g) \rightarrow 2CO_2(g)$	$2 \times (-394)$
$2CO_2(g) + 2H_2O(l) \rightarrow C_2H_4(g) + 3CO_2(g)$	$-(-1411)$
$2C(s) + 2H_2(g) \rightarrow C_2H_4(g)$	$+51$

(c) Enthalpy of atomization of ethene is:

$$-51 + 2\,(713) + 2\,(436) = 2246\ \text{kJ mol}^{-1}$$

Ethene contains 4 (C—H) bonds $= 4 \times 415 = 1660$ kJ mol^{-1}

$$\therefore \text{(C=C) bond energy} = 2247 - 1660$$
$$= 587\ \text{kJ mol}^{-1}$$

(d) The entropy decreases. Four moles of gas are converted to two moles of gas and two moles of liquid.

Example 2

For the reaction:

$$2H_2(g) + 2NO(g) \rightarrow 2H_2O(g) + N_2(g)$$

carried out at constant temperature the following data were obtained in three experiments.

Experiment	Initial concentration of NO (mol ℓ^{-1})	Initial concentration of H_2 (mol ℓ^{-1})	Initial rate of reaction (mol ℓ^{-1} s^{-1})
1	0.70	0.39	0.19
2	1.40	0.39	0.76
3	1.40	0.78	1.52

(a) Write the experimental rate expression with respect to (i) NO, (ii) H_2, *explaining* the terms used.

4 *marks*

(b) (i) Write the experiment rate law for the complete reaction.

(ii) What is the overall order of the reaction?'

3 *marks*

(c) Give an explanation why the overall order of the reaction cannot be obtained from the balanced equation for the reaction:

$$2H_2(g) + 2NO(g) \rightarrow 2H_2O(g) + N_2(g)$$

3 *marks*

(AEB: Nov 1980)

Answer

(a) **(i)** $Rate = K_1[NO]^2$

(ii) $Rate = K_2[H_2]$

Rate = rate of disappearance of reactant or appearance of product in mol ℓ^{-1} s^{-1}

K_1, K_2 are rate constants; [] = concentration in mol ℓ^{-1}.

(b) **(i)** $Rate = K[NO]^2[H_2]$

(ii) Third order.

(c) The equation gives the overall stoichiometry. It gives no information about the rate-determining step.

Example 3

Figure 11 shows the distribution of energy amongst molecules in a fixed amount of a gaseous mixture of hydrogen and iodine at a temperature *T*. The values plotted on the *y* axis are such that the area under the curve is proportional to the total number of molecules.

(a) Sketch on the diagram two curves, labelling them T_1 and T_2, showing the distribution of energies in a fixed mass of gas at a temperature T_1K which is appreciably less than TK and at a temperature T_2K which is appreciably greater than TK. 2 *marks*

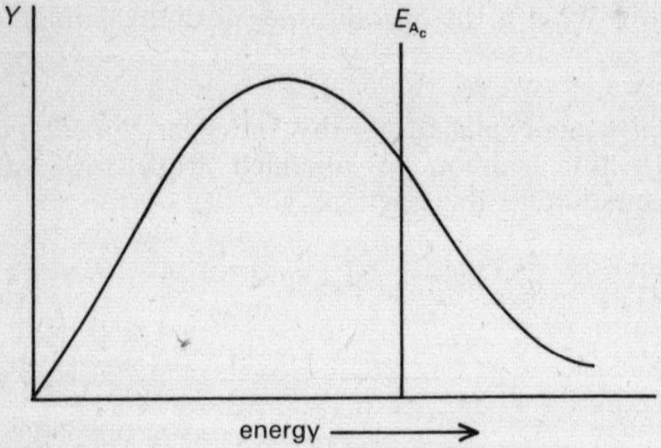

Figure 11

(b) E_{Ac} represents the activation energy for the reaction:

$H_2(g) + I_2(g) \rightarrow 2HI(g)$

(i) Define the term *activation energy*. 2 *marks*

(ii) How does the diagram help in understanding the effect of an increase in temperature on the rate of the reaction? 4 *marks*

(c) Name one factor, other than temperature, that may be used to change the rate of reaction between hydrogen and iodine. State the effect of this factor on the rate of the reaction. 2 *marks*

(AEB: June 1980)

Answer

(a) See Figure 12.

(b) **(i)** The minimum energy required by reactant molecules before reaction can occur.

(ii) The diagram shows that only a small fraction of reactant molecules need possess the activation energy before reaction can occur. Altering the temperature slightly has a great effect on the size of the fraction of molecules possessing E_{Ac} or more energy.

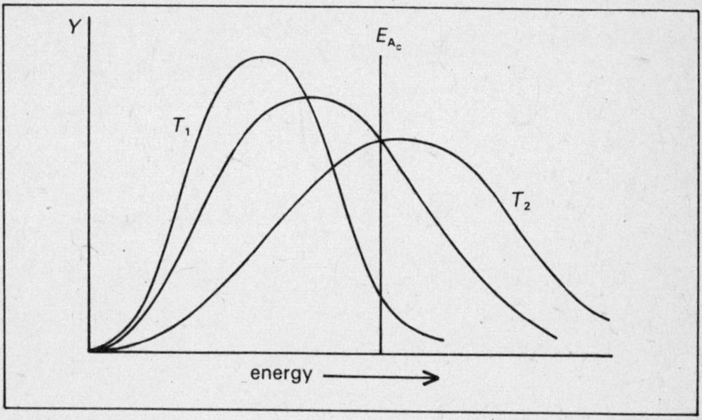

Figure 12

(c) Addition of a catalyst such as platinum. It increases the rate by adsorbing reactants and aiding reaction.

Example 4

(a) State Hess's law of constant heat summation (law of conservation of energy).

2 marks

(b) Define precisely the terms:

(i) enthalpy of formation (heat of formation).

2 marks

(ii) enthalpy of neutralization (heat of neutralization).

2 marks

(c) Using the data*, collected at 25°C and standard atmospheric pressure, in which the negative sign indicates heat evolved, calculate the enthalpy of formation of potassium chloride, KCl(s):

		ΔH(298K) kJ mol^{-1}
(i)	$KOH(aq) + HCl(aq) = KCl(aq) + H_2O(l)$	−57.3
(ii)	$H_2(g) + \frac{1}{2}O_2(g) = H_2O(l)$	−285.9
(iii)	$\frac{1}{2}H_2(g) + \frac{1}{2}Cl_2(g) + aq = HCl(aq)$	−164.2
(iv)	$K(s) + \frac{1}{2}O_2(g) + \frac{1}{2}H_2(g) + aq = KOH(aq)$	−487.0
(v)	$KCl(s) + aq = KCl(aq)$	+18.4

6 marks

*Candidates from certain schools may have used (c) instead of (s) to denote the solid (crystalline) state.

(Marks have been allocated for each step in the calculation, the numerical value of the answer carrying relatively few marks.)

(d) The enthalpy of neutralization of ethanoic acid (acetic acid) is −55.8 kJ mol^{-1} while that of hydrochloric acid is −57.3 kJ mol^{-1}, both reactions being with potassium hydroxide solution. Explain the difference in these two values and make what deductions you can.

6 marks

(SUJB part qu)

Answer

(a) The total enthalpy change accompanying a chemical reaction is independent of the path taken.

(b) **(i)** enthalpy change when one mole of a substance is formed from the elements in their standard state under standard conditions.

(ii) enthalpy change when one mole of a base or acid is completely neutralized under standard conditions.

(c)

	ΔH kJ mol^{-1}
$KOH(aq) + HCl(aq) = KCl(aq) + H_2O(l)$	-57.3
$K(s) + \frac{1}{2}O_2(g) + \frac{1}{2}H_2(g) + aq = KOH(aq)$	-487.0
$\frac{1}{2}H_2(g) + \frac{1}{2}Cl_2(g) + aq = HCl(aq)$	-164.2
$H_2O(l) = H_2(g) + \frac{1}{2}O_2(g)$	$-(-285.9)$
$KCl(aq) = KCl(s) + aq$	$-(+18.4)$
$\therefore K(s) + \frac{1}{2}Cl_2(g) = KCl(s)$	-441

(d) Both hydrochloric acid and potassium hydroxide are fully ionized. When one mole of any strong (fully ionized) monobasic acid and one mole of any strong monoacid base react the enthalpy change is a constant 57.3 kJ mol^{-1}. This is the enthalpy change of the reaction:

$$H^+ + OH^- = H_2O$$

If a weak acid (not fully ionized) such as ethanoic acid is neutralized the heat change will be less as one mole of acid produces less than one mole of water on neutralization.

Example 5

The following is a list of chemical reactions, each of which, under certain conditions, proceeds with the order shown.

A $2N_2O_5 \rightarrow 4NO_2 + O_2$ — First Order

B $CH_3COOH + C_2H_5OH \rightarrow CH_3COOC_2H_5 + H_2O$ — Second Order

C $2NO + O_2 \rightarrow 2NO_2$ — Third Order

(a) (i) Write a possible expression for the rate law of reaction C.

(ii) What is the probable order of reaction C with respect to NO?

2 marks

(b) In one experiment on reaction A, the initial concentration of N_2O_5 was 32 units and the half-life was 5 minutes. Plot the relation between the concentration of N_2O_5 and time for this experiment.

3 *marks*

(c) When the reaction A was carried out in tetrachloromethane, it was found that an initial concentration of N_2O_5 of 2.00 mol ℓ^{-1} gave an initial rate of reaction of 2.10×10^{-5} mol ℓ^{-1} s^{-1}. Calculate the rate constant for the reaction and state the units.

3 *marks*

(d) Given that reaction A is first order, suggest a mechanism to account for this.

3 *marks*

(e) Describe briefly how you would follow reaction B at 25°C.

5 *marks*

(L)

Answer

(a) (i) Rate $= K[NO]^2[O_2]$

(ii) Second order.

(b) See Figure 13.

(c) Rate $= K[N_2O_5]$ mol ℓ^{-1} s^{-1}

$$K = \frac{2.1 \times 10^{-5}}{2}$$

$$K = 1.05 \times 10^{-5}\ s^{-1}.$$

(d) $N_2O_5 \rightarrow 2NO_2 + O_2$ (slow)

$2O \rightarrow O_2$ (fast)

(e) Known initial amounts of ethyl ethanoate, water and

catalyst (hydrochloric acid) are allowed to stand at room temperature. After equilibrium is reached the mixture is titrated with alkali. After subtracting the volume of alkali required to neutralize the hydrochloric acid, the amount of ethanoic acid in the equilibrium mixture is calculated. From this concentrations of all reactants and products can be determined.

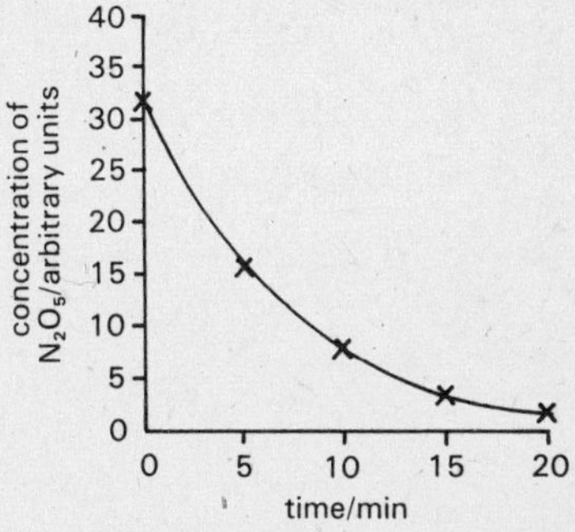

Figure 13

Example 6

This question uses the following data about boron and its compounds. On the graph (Figure 14) the number of electrons removed is plotted against the logarithm of the appropriate ionization energy and in the table standard enthalpy changes are listed for various processes.

Process	$\Delta H^{\ominus}_{298}$/kJ mol^{-1}
First electron affinity of oxygen	−140
Second electron affinity of oxygen	+790
Standard heat of atomization of oxygen	+250
Standard heat of atomization of boron	+590

Standard heat of formation of the oxide of boron	−1270
First ionization energy of boron	+800
Second ionization energy of boron	+2400
Third ionization energy of boron	+3700
Fourth ionization energy of boron	+25 000
Fifth ionization energy of boron	+32 800

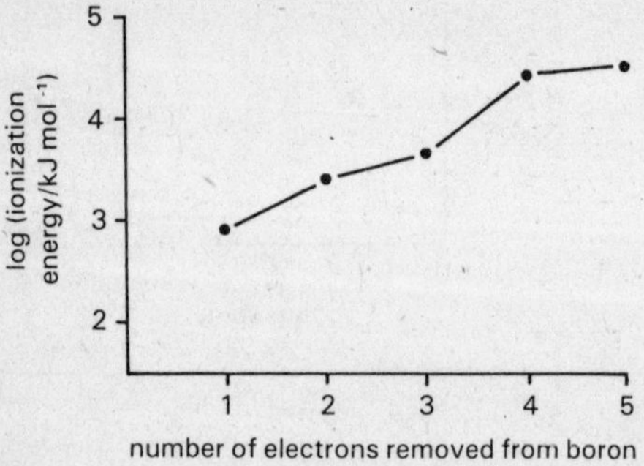

Figure 14

(a) (i) On the graph, label each point with the electronic configuration (*s*, *p*, *d* or *f*) of the corresponding electron.

(ii) Deduce the most likely formula for the oxide of boron. *3 marks*

(b) (i) Draw a labelled Born–Haber cycle for the formation of the oxide of boron (assumed to be ionic).

(ii) Calculate a lattice energy for the oxide of boron. *5 marks*

(c) (i) One mole of the oxide of boron reacts with three moles of water and the product dissolves in water to give a weakly acidic solution. Write an equation, with state symbols, for the equilibrium occurring in aqueous solution.

(ii) Would you expect your value for the lattice energy of the oxide of boron to be in good or poor agreement with a theoretically derived value? Give your reason(s).

4 *marks*
(NUFF)

Answer

(a) (i) See Figure 15.

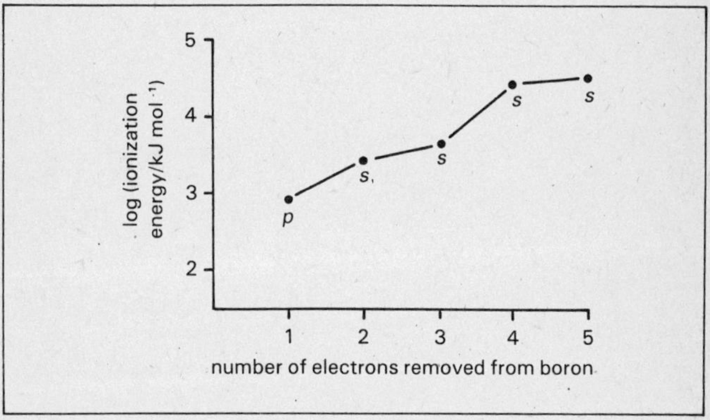

Figure 15

(ii) B_2O_3.

(b) (i) See Figure 16.

(ii) $U = -(2 \times 590 + 3 \times 250 + 2 \times 6900 + 3 \times 650) - 1270$

$= -18\,950\ \text{kJ mol}^{-1}$

(c) (i) $B_2O_3(s) + 3H_2O(l) \rightleftharpoons 6H^+(aq) + 2BO_3^{2-}(aq)$

(ii) Poor agreement. It is assumed that the oxide is fully ionic but it must have considerable covalent character.

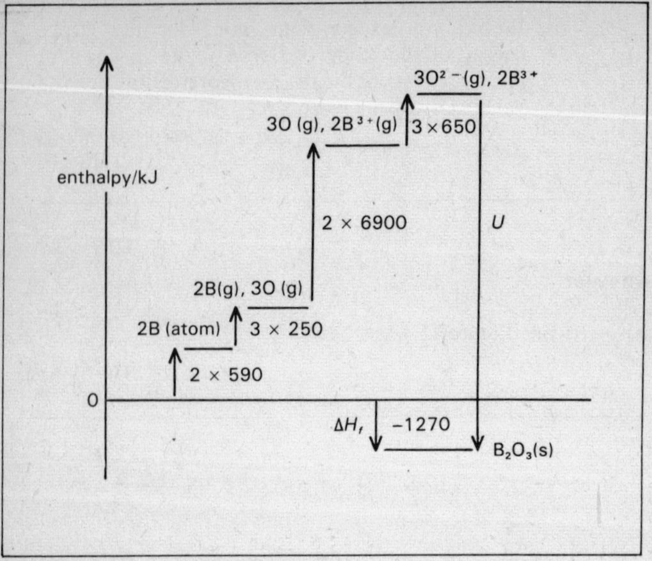

Figure 16

Example 7

You may need to refer to some or all of the information in Figure 17 in answering this question.

$\Delta H^\ominus(\text{atomization})_{298}$ [C(graphite)] $= +715\,\text{kJ mol}^{-1}$

Mean bond energies: $E(\text{C—C}) = +346\,\text{kJ mol}^{-1}$
$E(\text{C—H}) = +413\,\text{kJ mol}^{-1}$

The enthalpy changes listed below refer to the quantities indicated in the equations.

$3C(\text{graphite}) + 4H_2(g) \longrightarrow 3C(g) + 8H(g)$ $\quad \Delta H_1^\ominus = +3889\,\text{kJ mol}^{-1}$

$3C(g) + 8H(g) \longrightarrow C_3H_6(g) + H_2(g) \quad \Delta H_2^\ominus = ?$

$3C(graphite) + 4H_2(g) \rightarrow C_3H_6(g)$ $\Delta H_3^{\ominus} = ?$

$C_3H_8(g) \rightarrow C_3H_6(g) + H_2(g)$ $\Delta H_4^{\ominus} = +124\,\text{kJ mol}^{-1}$

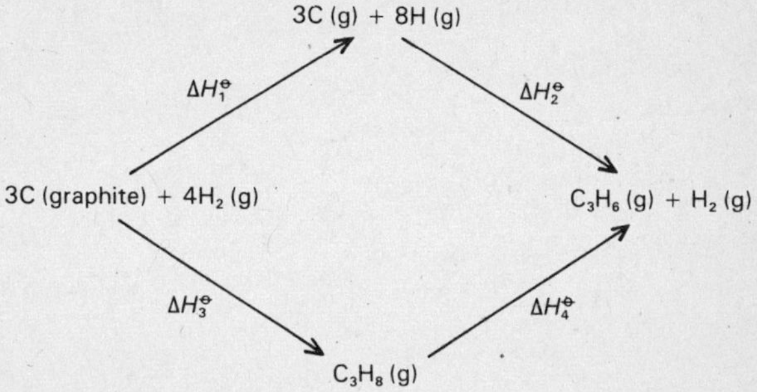

Figure 17

(a) On what law is the above energy cycle based?
1 *mark*

(b) What name is given to the energy change $\Delta H_3^{\ominus}$?
1 *mark*

(c) Calculate a value for the standard enthalpy change of atomization of hydrogen $\Delta H^{\ominus}(\text{atomization})_{298}$ $[\frac{1}{2}H_2(g)]$.
3 *marks*

(d) Calculate an approximate value, using mean bond energy terms, for the enthalpy change of atomization of propane, $C_3H_8(g)$.
2 *marks*

(e) (i) Using the energy values calculated in (c) and (d) and any other relevant data, draw an energy cycle in order to determine the standard enthalpy change of atomization of propene, $C_3H_6(g)$, at 298K. Then calculate a value for this enthalpy change.

(ii) Hence calculate an approximate value for the mean bond energy of the C═C bond, *E*(C═C).
6 *marks*
(NUFF)

Answer

(a) Hess's Law.

(b) Standard enthalpy of formation of propane.

(c) $\Delta H^{\ominus}$ atom$[\frac{1}{2}\text{H(g)}] = \frac{1}{8}(\Delta H_1^{\ominus} - 3 \times \Delta H^{\ominus}$ atom[C(s)]

$$= \tfrac{1}{8}(3889 - 3 \times 715)$$

$$= 218 \text{ kJ mol}^{-1}$$

(d) $2 \times E(\text{C—C}) = 2 \times 346 \text{ kJ}$

$8 \times E(\text{C—H}) = 8 \times 413 \text{ kJ}$

Total energy $= 3996 \text{ kJ mol}^{-1}$.

(e) **(i)** See Figure 18.

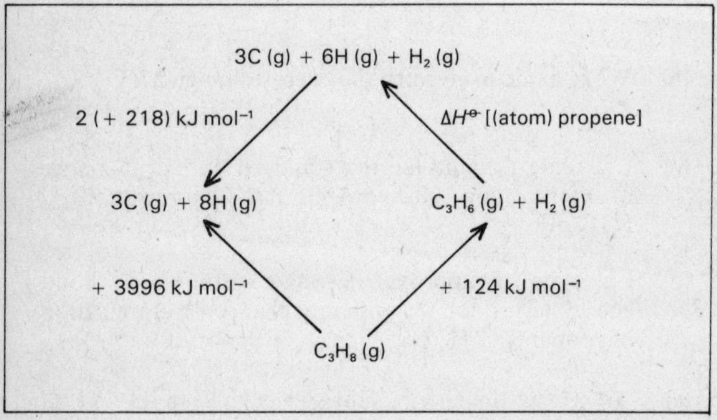

Figure 18

$$\Delta H^{\ominus}(\text{atomization})_{\textbf{propene}} = -(124) + 3996 - 2 \times (218)$$
$$= 3426 \text{ kJ mol}^{-1}.$$

(ii) $1 \times E(\text{C—C}) = +346 \text{ kJ}$

$6 \times E(\text{C—H}) = 6 \times 413 \text{ kJ}$

Total $= 2824 \text{ kJ}$

$\therefore E(\text{C=C}) = 3436 - 2824 = 612 \text{ kJ mol}^{-1}$

Chapter 5

Electrochemistry and ionic equilibria

Example 1

Explain fully what is meant by the term *solubility product*, indicating the limitations on its use, and derive an expression for the solubility product of the salt A_3B_2 given that its solubility in water is S mol ℓ^{-1}. 10 *marks*

(a) Calculate the solubility of silver iodide ($g\,\ell^{-1}$) in water given that the numerical value of its solubility product is 1.0×10^{-16} [Mr(AgI) = 235]. 5 *marks*

(b) Calculate the solubility product of lead iodide, stating the units in which it is expressed, given that the solubility in water is $6.04 \times 10^{-1}\,g\,\ell^{-1}$ [Mr(PbI_2) = 461]. 5 *marks*

(c) If solid potassium iodide (which is freely soluble in water) is added in minute quantities at a time to a solution which is 0.02 M in both lead(II) nitrate, $Pb(NO_3)_2$ and silver nitrate, $AgNO_3$:

(i) which of the cations is precipitated first?

(ii) what will be its concentration (mol ℓ^{-1}) when the second cation begins to be precipitated?

10 *marks*

(SUJB)

Answer

Solubility product applies to solutions of sparingly soluble electrolytes at constant temperature. It is a constant which is derived by applying the equilibrium law:

$$A_3B_2(s) + aq \rightleftharpoons 3A^{2+}(aq) + 2B^{3-}(aq)$$

$$K=\frac{[A^{2+}(aq)]^3[B^{3-}(aq)]^2}{[A_3B_2(s)]}$$

$[A_3B_2(s)]$ is constant.

$\therefore\ K_{sp}=[A^{2+}(aq)]^3[B^{3-}(aq)]^2$

If S mol ℓ^{-1} of A_3B_2 dissolve then $[A^{2+}(aq)]=3S$ and $[B^{3-}(aq)]=2S$ mol ℓ^{-1}

$\therefore\ K_{sp}=(3S)^3(2S)^2$

$K_{sp}=108S^5\ \text{mol}^5\ \ell^{-5}$

(a) For AgI $K_{sp}=1.0\times10^{-16}$ mol ℓ^{-1}.

$\therefore\ 1.0\times10^{-16}=[Ag^+(aq)][I^-(aq)]$

If the solubility of AgI is x mol ℓ^{-1} then:

$[Ag^+(aq)] \quad =[I^-(aq)]=x$

$\therefore\ 1.0\times10^{-16} \quad =x^2$

$\therefore\ x \quad =10^{-8}$ mol ℓ^{-1}

Mr(AgI) $\quad =235$

$\therefore$ solubility of AgI $=235\times10^{-8}$

$=2.35\times10^{-6}\ \text{g}\ \ell^{-1}$

(b) Solubility of $PbI_2=6.04\times10^{-1}\ \text{g}\ \ell^{-1}$

$$=\frac{6.04\times10^{-1}}{461}\ \text{mol}\ \ell^{-1}$$

$K_{sp}=[Pb^{2+}(aq)][I^-(aq)]^2$

$$K_{sp} = \left(\frac{6.04 \times 10^{-1}}{461}\right)\left(\frac{2 \times 6.04 \times 10^{-1}}{461}\right)^2$$

$$K_{sp} = 9 \times 10^{-9}\ \text{mol}^3\ \ell^{-3}$$

(c) (i) Silver.

(ii) When PbI_2 begins to be precipitated:

$$[Pb^{2+}(aq)] = 2 \times 10^{-2}\ \text{mol}\ \ell^{-1}$$

$$\therefore [I^-(aq)]^2 = \frac{K_{sp}}{[Pb^{2+}(aq)]}$$

$$= \frac{9 \times 10^{-9}}{2 \times 10^{-2}}$$

$$= 4.5 \times 10^{-7}$$

$$[I^-(aq)] = 6.7 \times 10^{-4}\ \text{mol}\ \ell^{-1}$$

$$[Ag^+(aq)] = \frac{K_{sp}}{[I^-(aq)]}$$

$$= \frac{10^{-16}}{6.7 \times 10^{-4}}$$

$\therefore$ Concentration of silver ion $= 1.5 \times 10^{-12}\ \text{mol}\ \ell^{-1}$.

Example 2

A student conducted an experiment to determine the solubility product of silver chloride using the apparatus represented in Figure 19. The emf measured was -0.12 V.

The potential of the silver electrode in a solution of silver ions is given by the equation:

$E = E^{\ominus} + 0.06 \log_{10} [Ag^+]$.

(a) The standard electrode potential of silver is $+0.80$ V. What do you understand by this?

2 marks

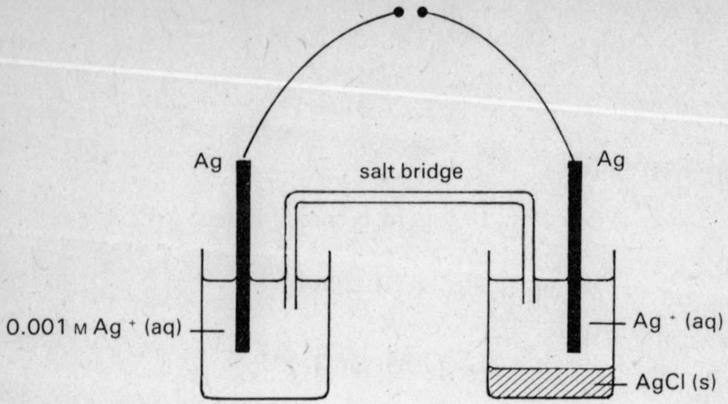

Figure 19

(b) Using the above equation, derive an expression for the emf found in this experiment.

2 *marks*

(c) Calculate the concentration of silver ions in the right-hand half-cell.

3 *marks*

(d) (i) Write an expression for the solubility product of silver chloride.

Calculate its value.

(ii) What is the purpose of the solid silver chloride in the right-hand half-cell?

3 *marks*

(e) How would you prepare a salt bridge for this experiment.

1 *mark*

(f) How would you expect the emf to change if a few drops of aqueous sodium chloride were added to the right-hand half-cell? Explain your answer.

3 *marks*

(L)

Answer

(a) When a silver electrode in an aqueous solution of molar silver ions at 298K is connected via a voltmeter to a standard hydrogen electrode the voltmeter will read 0.8 V. The silver electrode is positive.

(b) emf $= E(\text{rhs}) - E(\text{lhs})$

$= E^{\ominus} + 0.06\log_{10}[Ag^+] - E^{\ominus} - 0.06\log_{10}(10^{-3})$

E $= 0.06\log_{10}[Ag^+] - 0.06\log_{10}(10^{-3})$

(c) $-0.12 = 0.06\log_{10}[Ag^+] - 0.06(-3)$

$-2 = \log_{10}[Ag^+] + 3$

$\log_{10}[Ag^+] = -5$

$[Ag^+] = 10^{-5}\ \text{mol}\ \ell^{-1}$

(d) (i) $K_{sp} = [Ag^+(aq)]_{eqm}[Cl^-(aq)]_{eqm}$

$K_{sp} = 10^{-5} \times 10^{-5}$

$K_{sp} = 10^{-10}\ \text{mol}^2\ \ell^{-2}$

(**ii**) To maintain a saturated solution.

(e) Filter paper soaked in a solution of a salt containing unreactive ions.

(f) It would decrease (more negative) because the increased concentration of chloride ions would cause more silver ions to precipitate and lower $[Ag^+(aq)]$ and E(rhs) would decrease.

Example 3

This question is about the redox reaction between MnO_4^- ions and Fe^{2+} ions.

$$MnO_4^-(aq) + 8H^+(aq) + 5e^- \rightleftharpoons Mn^{2+}(aq) + 4H_2O(l) \qquad E^{\ominus} = +1.51\ \text{V}$$

$$Fe^{3+}(aq) + e^- \rightleftharpoons Fe^{2+}(aq) \qquad E^{\ominus} = +0.77\ \text{V}$$

(a) Draw and label *fully* a diagram of the apparatus you could use to measure the standard electrode potential of the Fe^{3+}(aq), Fe^{2+}(aq) half-cell. Be careful to mention all *necessary conditions* (concentration, temperature, electrodes, etc). 5 *marks*

(b) (i) What are the changes in oxidation number when Fe^{2+}(aq) and MnO_4^-(aq) react in acidic solution?

(ii) Hence write a balanced equation for the reaction. 4 *marks*

(c) (i) Write out a cell diagram for the system Fe^{3+}(aq), Fe^{2+}(aq) linked with the system MnO_4^-(aq), Mn^{2+}(aq) in standard conditions.

(ii) What would be the emf of this cell?

(iii) Which would be the positive electrode?

(iv) The relationship between $E^{\ominus}_{cell}$ and K_c at 298K is:

$$E^{\ominus}_{cell} = \frac{2.3\,RT}{zF} \log K_c$$

Calculate K_c for the reaction of Fe^{2+}(aq) with MnO_4^-(aq) in standard conditions.

($R = 8.31\ \mathrm{J\,K^{-1}\,mol^{-1}}$, $F = 96\,500\ \mathrm{C\,mol^{-1}}$).

7 *marks*

(NUFF)

Answer

(a) See Figure 20.

(b) **(i)** Iron: +2 to +3.
Manganese: +7 to +2.

(ii) $5Fe^{2+}(aq) + MnO_4^-(aq) + 8H^+(aq) \rightarrow 5Fe^{3+}(aq) + Mn^{2+}(aq) + 4H_2O(l)$

(c) **(i)** Pt/Fe^{2+}(aq), Fe^{3+}(aq) ¦ MnO_4^-(aq), Mn^{2+}(aq)/Pt

(ii) $E = 1.51 - 0.77 = +0.74\ \mathrm{V}$

(iii) MnO_4^-(aq), Mn^{2+}(aq)/Pt.

(iv) $\log K_c = \dfrac{E^{\ominus}_{cell} \times z \times F}{2.3 \times R \times T}$

$$K_c = \frac{0.74 \times 5 \times 96\,500}{2.3 \times 8.31 \times 298} = 10^{63}$$

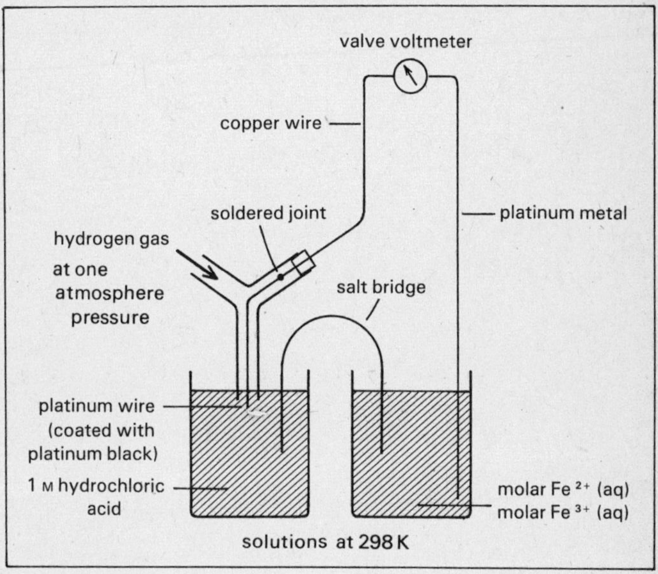

Figure 20

Example 4

This question concerns the changes which take place when a 0.1 M solution of sodium hydroxide is added to 25 cm^3 of 0.1 M hydrochloric acid.

In three separate experiments changes in temperature, pH and electrical conductivity were measured using a thermometer, a pH electrode and a conductivity dip cell, respectively.

(a) On the axes in Figure 21, sketch the relationship between volume of alkali added and each of the properties measured. 6 *marks*

(b) On the same axes, use broken lines (- - - -) to indicate the results you would expect if 0.1 M ethanoic acid were used instead of hydrochloric acid. 3 *marks*

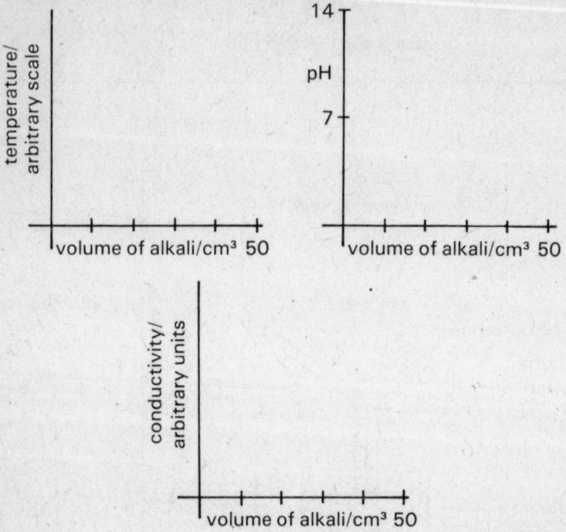

Figure 21

(c) State, with reasons, which indicator you would use in titrating sodium hydroxide with:

(i) hydrochloric acid.

(ii) ethanoic acid. 4 *marks*

(d) If the molar enthalpy of neutralization for hydrochloric acid by sodium hydroxide is $57\,kJ\,mol^{-1}$, calculate the maximum temperature change expected during the titration described in (a). Assume that the specific heat capacity of all solutions is $4.2\,JK^{-1}\,cm^{-3}$. 2 *marks*

(L)

Answer

(a) See Figure 22.

(b) See Figure 22.

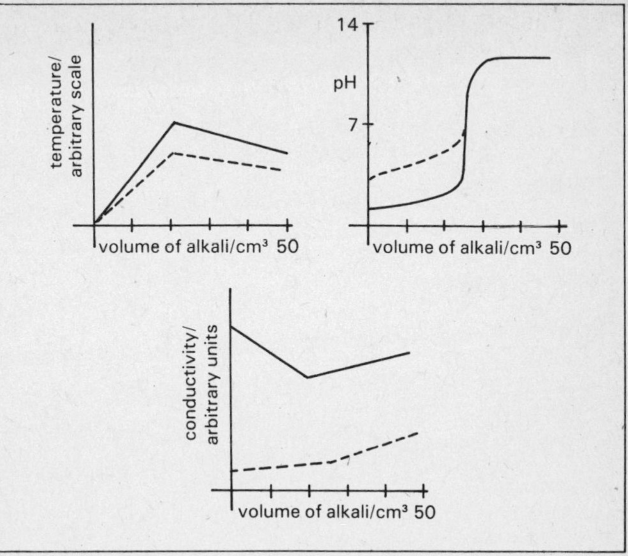

Figure 22

(c) (i) Any suitable indicator, eg, methyl orange. At equivalence point, pH changes from 3 to 11 rapidly, and so most indicators will change colour.

(ii) Phenolphthalein. At equivalence point the rapid pH change is on the alkaline side of 7. Phenolphthalein changes around pH 10.

(d) Heat change = mass × specific heat × temp. rise.

$$\text{Amount of acid} = 0.1 \times \frac{25}{100} \text{ moles}$$

$$\therefore \text{ Heat change} = 2.5 \times 10^{-4} \times 57 \times 10^{3}\ \text{J}$$

$$\text{Temp. rise} = \frac{\text{Heat change}}{2.5 \times 10^{-4} \times 57 \times 10^{3}}$$

$$\text{Temp. rise} = \frac{25 \times 57 \times 10^{-1}}{50 \times 4.2}$$

$$= 0.68^{\circ}\text{C}$$

Example 5

Define the term pH. *2 marks*

(a) Write an expression for the acidity constant (acid ionization constant, dissociation constant), K_a, of ethanoic acid (acetic acid), $CH_3.COOH$, given that

$K_a = 1.8 \times 10^{-5}\,\text{mol}\,\ell^{-1}$ at 291K. *1 mark*

(b) Explain what is understood by the term pK_a and calculate its value for ethanoic acid.

3 marks

(c) Calculate the percentage ionization (mol %) of ethanoic acid in a 0.1 M solution of the acid at 291K.

5 marks

(d) Sketch a titration curve to show the pH change (vertical axis) which occurs on adding $30\,\text{cm}^3$ 0.1 M sodium hydroxide solution to $25\,\text{cm}^3$ 0.1 M ethanoic acid at 291K. The pH of the acid should be calculated initially and after addition of 5, 12.5, 20 and $30\,\text{cm}^3$ of alkali.

13 marks

(e) What is a buffer solution? Give at least one example, with an indication of the molar proportions of the mixture. Relate what you have described to the titration curve in (d) and indicate where you consider buffer capacity to be a maximum. Explain your opinion.

6 marks

(SUJB)

Answer

pH is negative $\log_{10}$ [hydrogen ion concentration].

(a) $K_a = \dfrac{[H^+][CH_3COO^-]}{[CH_3COOH]} = 1.8 \times 10^{-5}\,\text{mol}\,\ell^{-1}$

(b) $\mathrm{p}K_a = -\log_{10}(K_a)$.

For ethanoic acid $\mathrm{p}K_a = -\log_{10}(1.8 \times 10^{-5})$

$$= 4.74$$

(c) $K_a \quad = \dfrac{\alpha^2}{(1-\alpha)V}$ where α is the degree of ionization

$K_a \quad \sim \dfrac{\alpha^2}{V}$ and V is the dilution in ℓ per mol.

$\therefore \alpha \quad = \sqrt{(K_a V)}$

For 0.1 M ethanoic acid:

$\alpha \quad = \sqrt{(1.8 \times 10^{-5} \times 10)}$

$\alpha \quad = 0.013$

$\therefore$ 0.1 M ethanoic acid is 1.3% ionized.

(d) Initial pH of acid:

$[H^+] = \sqrt{(K_a C)}$ where C = acid concentration.

$= \sqrt{(1.8 \times 10^{-5} \times 10^{-1})}$M

$\therefore$ pH = 2.87

pH after addition of 5 cm^3 of alkali:

5 cm^3 of acid react with the alkali leaving 20 cm^3 of acid in a total volume of 30 cm^3.

$\therefore$ Concentration of acid $= \dfrac{20}{30} \times 0.1 = 0.067$ M

$[H^+] = \sqrt{(1.8 \times 10^{-5} \times 0.067)}$M

$\therefore$ pH = 2.96

pH after addition of 12.5 cm^3 of alkali:

$$[H^+] = \sqrt{\left(1.8 \times 10^{-5} \times 0.1 \times \frac{12.5}{37.5}\right)} \text{ M}$$

$$\therefore \text{pH} = 3.1$$

pH after addition of 20 cm^3 of alkali:

$$[H^+] = \sqrt{\left(1.8 \times 10^{-5} \times 0.1 \times \frac{5}{45}\right)} \text{ M}$$

$$\therefore \text{pH} = 3.34$$

pH after the addition of 30 cm^3 of alkali:

All the acid has reacted, leaving 5 cm^3 of alkali in 55 cm^3 of solution

$$[OH^-] = \frac{5}{55} \times 0.1 \text{ M}$$

$$\therefore \text{pOH} = 2.04$$

$$\therefore \text{pH} = 11.96$$

For titration curve see Figure 23.

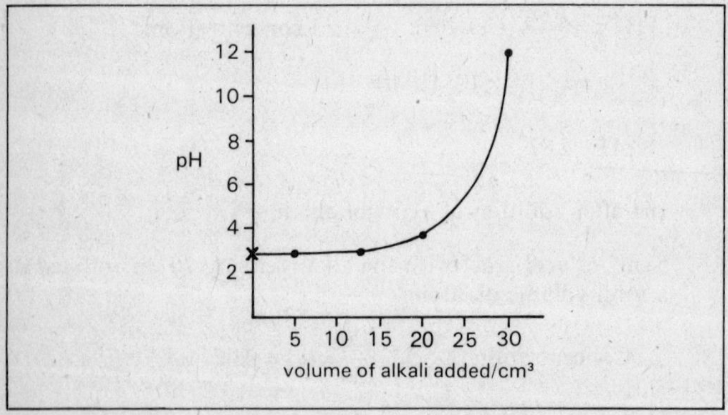

Figure 23

(e) A buffer solution is a mixture of a weak acid with a salt of the acid or a weak base with a salt of the base. Example: sodium ethanoate with ethanoic acid in equimolar proportions. A buffer solution controls pH. In the titration in (d), the solution before the end-point contains sodium ethanoate and ethanoic acid. As sodium hydroxide is added (up to $20\,cm^3$) the pH changes gradually. The solution is acting as a buffer over the horizontal part of the curve up to $20\,cm^3$ NaOH added. Beyond this point the pH starts to increase rapidly.

Example 6

This question is about the measurement of pH and the properties of the buffer solution obtained by mixing ethanoic acid and sodium ethanoate.

(a) Draw and label a diagram of an electrode system that can be used to measure pH. 4 *marks*

(b) Would the pH be above or below pH 7 in an aqueous mixture of ethanoic acid and sodium ethanoate? 1 *mark*

(c) Describe the changes in pH and composition of the mixture which would occur on the addition of a *small amount* of:

(i) dilute aqueous hydrochloric acid.

(ii) dilute aqueous sodium hydroxide. 4 *marks*

(d) Use the relationship:

$$pH = pK_a - \log\frac{[acid]}{[base]}$$

to calculate the pH of a mixture of 0.4 M ethanoic acid with 0.2 M sodium ethanoate in equal volumes. (For ethanoic acid, $pK_a = 4.8$). 2 *marks*

(e) Name a biochemical system in which buffer action is important. 1 *mark*

(NUFF)

Answer

(a) See Figure 24.

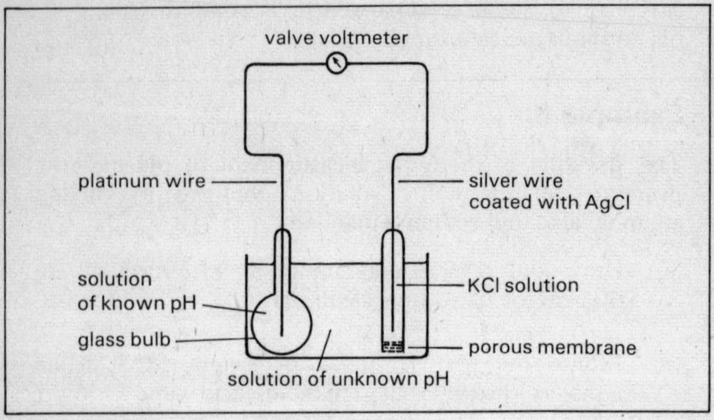

Figure 24

(b) Below pH 7.

(c) (i) Almost no change in pH. The hydrogen ions react with the large reservoir of ethanoate ions and form ethanoic acid. The amount of ethanoic acid is slightly increased and the amount of sodium ethanoate slightly reduced.

(ii) Almost no change in pH. The hydroxide ion reacts with hydrogen ions to form water. Some ethanoic acid will dissociate to make up the hydrogen ion concentration to its former level.

(d) $pH = 4.8 - \log\frac{0.4}{0.2}$

$= 4.8 - 0.301 = 4.5$

(e) Blood.

Example 7

Ethanoic acid is a weak acid with a pK_a value of 4.74 at 298K.

(a) (i) What do you understand by the terms pK_a and K_a?

(ii) Calculate the numerical value of K_a for ethanoic acid.

3 marks

(b) Calculate the pH value of 298K of:

(i) a 1.0 M solution of ethanoic acid.

(ii) a mixture of equal volumes of 1.0 M solutions of ethanoic acid and sodium ethanoate.

5 marks

(c) The solution in (b) (ii) is a buffer solution.

(i) Give another example of a buffer solution.

(ii) What is the main characteristic of buffer solutions?

(iii) Give TWO uses of buffer solutions, or instances where they are important.

4 *marks*)

(L)

Answer

(a) **(i)** $pK_a = -\log_{10} K_a$

K_a is the acid dissociation constant.

For ethanoic acid $K_a = \dfrac{[H^+][CH_3COO^-]}{[CH_3COOH]}$

(ii) K_a = antilog (-4.74)

$= 1.8 \times 10^{-5}\ \text{mol}\ \ell^{-1}$

(b) (i) $[H^+]=\sqrt{(K_aC)}$ where C = concentration of acid.

$$[H^+]=\sqrt{(1.8\times10^{-5}\times1)}$$

$$=4.24\times10^{-3}$$

$\therefore$ pH = 2.37

(ii) $$pH=pK_a-\log_{10}\frac{[acid]}{[base]}$$

$$=4.74-\log\frac{1}{1}$$

pH = 4.74

(c) (i) Ammonium chloride and aqueous ammonia.

(ii) Controls the pH. Adding small quantities of acid or base does not alter pH greatly.

(iii) Blood is buffered, since a slight alteration in its pH would greatly affect biochemical reactions. A buffer solution is used as a reference standard for measuring pH of test solutions in a pH meter.

Example 8

(a) Write an expression which represents the ionic product of water. Explain the symbols used.

4 marks

(b) The ionic product for water at 25°C is 1.00×10^{-14} mol^2 ℓ^{-2}; and at 50°C it is 5.48×10^{-14} mol^2 ℓ^{-2}. Calculate the hydrogen ion concentration in pure water at (i) 25°C and (ii) 50°C. (iii) State any assumption(s) you make.

3 marks

(c) Use your results from (b) to state how:

(i) the ionization of water ($H_2O \rightleftharpoons H^+(aq) + OH^-(aq)$),

(ii) the pH of water,

change with increasing temperature. *3 marks*

(AEB: Nov 1980)

Answer

(a) $K_w = [H^+][OH^-]\,mol^2\,\ell^{-2}$.

K_w = ionic product

$[H^+]$, $[OH^-]$ are the concentrations of hydrogen ions and hydroxide ions, respectively.

(b) (i) $[H^+] = [OH^-] = K_w$

at 25°C, $[H^+] = \sqrt{10^{-14}} = 10^{-7}\,mol\,\ell^{-1}$.

(ii) at 50°C, $[H^+] = \sqrt{(5.48 \times 10^{-14})} = 2.3 \times 10^{-7}\,mol\,\ell^{-1}$.

(iii) Hydrogen ion concentration is equal to hydroxide ion concentration. The concentration of undissociated water is constant.

(c) (i) Ionization increases with increasing temperature.

(ii) pH increases with increasing temperature.

Chapter 6

Atomic structure, bonding and quantitative analysis

Example 1

(a) Define the terms *first ionization energy* and *second ionization energy*, illustrating your answer with an equation in each case.

(i) First ionization energy is:

Equation:

(ii) Second ionization energy is:

Equation: *4 marks*

(b) Sketch the relationship between log of successive ionization energies and ionization number for the element aluminium, atomic number 13. *2 marks*

(c) The third ionization energy of magnesium is approximately ten times the first ionization energy and five times the second.

Explain:

(i) Why successive ionization energies increase with ionization number.

(ii) Why, in the case of magnesium, the third ionization energy is *much* higher than the first two. *3 marks*

(d) The graph in Figure 25 is a plot of first ionization energy against atomic number for nine consecutive elements in the Periodic Table.

(i) Give the names of the first and last elements to which the graph might refer.

(ii) Explain briefly the shape of the graph. *5 marks*

(L)

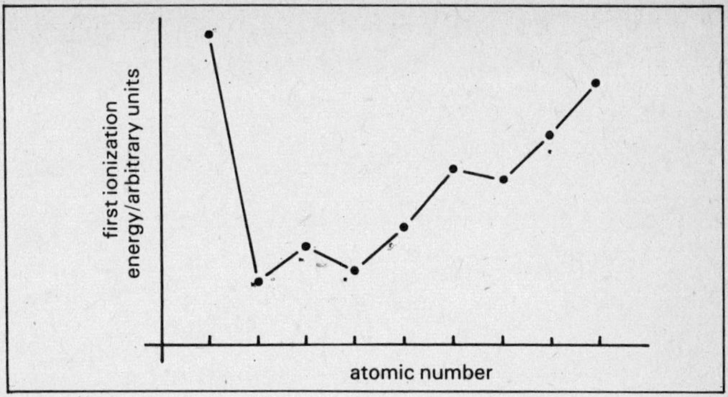

Figure 25

Answer

(a) **(i)** First ionization energy is the energy required to remove 1 mol of electrons from 1 mol of free gaseous atoms of the element to produce 1 mol of monopositive ions:

Equation: $M(g) \rightarrow M(g)^{+} + e^{-}$

(ii) Second ionization energy is the energy required to remove 1 mol of electrons from 1 mol of monopositive ions of the element.

Equation: $M^{+}(g) \rightarrow M^{2+}(g) + e^{-}$

(b) See Figure 26.

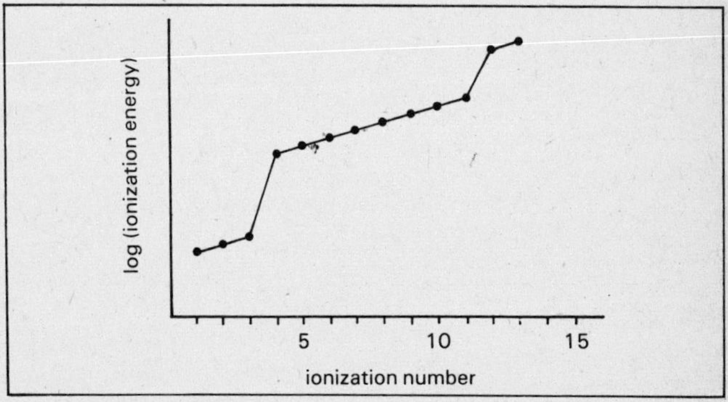

Figure 26

(c) (i) This is because once an electron is lost there is a greater imbalance between the charges on the remaining electrons and that on the nucleus, hence these remaining electrons are held more firmly.

(ii) The second electron is lost from an incomplete 3*s* orbital but the third is lost from a stable $2s^2 2p^6$ configuration.

(d) (i) The first element could be helium (or neon). The last element could be fluorine (or chlorine).

(ii) A noble gas has a stable $ns^2 np^6$ configuration (ns^2 for helium); hence they are at peaks in the graph. For the other elements, there is a general increase with increasing atomic number owing to the extra protons in the nucleus increasing the attraction for electrons. Minor peaks occur corresponding to a filled ns^2 orbital and a half filled *p* orbital (np^3) indicating the stability associated with these arrangements.

Example 2

(a) The diagram in Figure 27 represents the atomic emission spectrum of hydrogen.

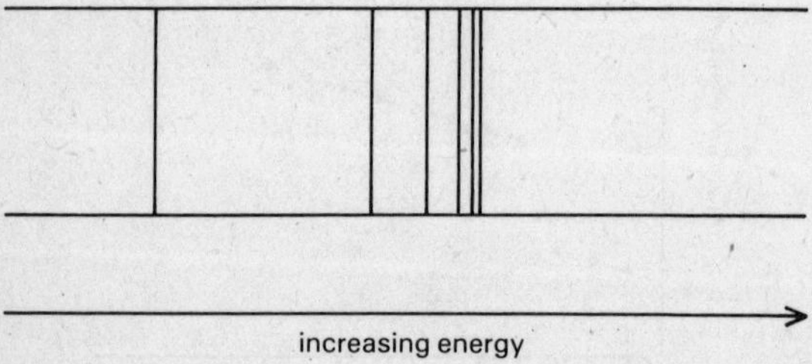

Figure 27

(i) Explain why the spectrum is composed of lines rather than being continuous. *2 marks*

(ii) What does each line indicate? *1 mark*

(iii) Explain why the lines become progressively closer to each other. *2 marks*

(b) Sodium hydride contains hydrogen in the form of an ion.

(i) In terms of electronic structures explain the formation of sodium hydride. *2 marks*

(ii) What is the evidence for the existence of the hydride ion? *2 marks*

(iii) Sodium hydride is a crystalline compound with 6:6 co-ordination. Describe a possible crystal structure for sodium hydride. *3 marks*

(AEB: June 1979)

Answer

(a) **(i)** The spectrum consists of lines as each represents a definite energy change associated with transfer of an electron from one orbital to another.

(ii) Each line represents a different transition of an electron from one particular orbital to another particular orbital.

(iii) This is because the energy difference between higher orbitals is less than for transitions involving lower orbitals. Thus the energy difference between the first and second orbital is greater than that between the second and third and so on.

(b) **(i)**

Na +	H	*Atom*
(2.8.1)	(1)	(Electron arrangement of atom)
$\downarrow -e^-$	$\downarrow +e^-$	
Na^+	H^-	*Ion*
(2.8.0)	(2)	(Electron arrangement of ion)

(ii) The product is an ionic solid that on electrolysis of the fused salt produces hydrogen at the anode:

$2H^- \rightarrow H_2 + 2e^-$

(iii) It would adopt a sodium chloride lattice, in which each sodium ion would be surrounded by six hydride ions (2 each along the *x*, *y* and *z* axes) and vice versa.

Example 3

An element *Q* has the electronic configuration:

$1s^2 2s^2 2p^6 3s^2 3p^6 4s^2 3d^{10} 4p^1$.

(a) Write down the atomic number of *Q*. 2 *marks*

(b) *Q* occurs naturally as a mixture of ^{69}Q and ^{71}Q. Explain the significance of the numbers 69 and 71, and say what these two components in the natural element are called. 5 *marks*

(c) If ^{69}Q and ^{71}Q occur in the proportions 60.0% and 40.0%, respectively, calculate the relative atomic mass of *Q*. 4 *marks*

(d) Assign a group of the Periodic Table to *Q* and explain your answer. 3 *marks*

(e) Explain why the oxidation state of *Q* is always +3. 2 *marks*

(f) Write down the formula of the oxide of *Q* and comment on its acidic/basic character in comparison with the oxides of the elements higher in the same group of the Periodic Table. 4 *marks*

(g) *Q*(III) chloride is a dimer under certain conditions. Suggest a structure for this chloride. 4 *marks*

(SUJB)

Answer

(a) *Q* has the atomic number 31.

(b) These numbers are the mass numbers of the atoms, indicating the total of neutrons + protons in the nucleus. These two components, called isotopes as they have the same atomic number but different mass number, both contain 31 protons, the higher isotope having 38 neutrons, the heavier 40 neutrons.

(c) $Ar(Q) = \frac{(6 \times 69) + (4 \times 71)}{10} = \frac{414 + 284}{10} = 69.8$

(d) Q is in Group III of the Periodic Table as it has the outer electron configuration ns^2np^1, ie, it has 3 electrons in its outer orbital (the $3d^{10}$ orbital is in the penultimate shell).

(e) Q will form ions Q^{3+} by loss of the $4s^2$ and $4p^1$ electrons. To lose any fewer would not leave a stable electron arrangement. To lose more would involve using electrons from the filled $3d^{10}$ orbital, and would thus require too much energy.

(f) The oxide would be Q_2O_3. It would be weakly basic, not amphoteric as is Al_2O_3 as going down a group in the Periodic Table results in increased basic (and hence less acidic) character.

(g) The dimer would probably have the structure:

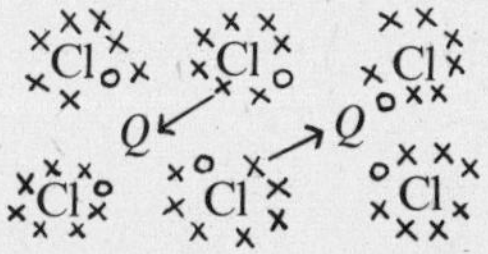

Example 4

Figure 28 represents a part of the Periodic Table with some elements denoted by the letters A to K. The letters do not represent the chemical symbols of the elements.

Answer the following questions by reference to the letters A to K.

(a) (i) Select an element forming compounds in which it occurs in two oxidation states.

(ii) Write formulae for the oxides of this element.
2 *marks*

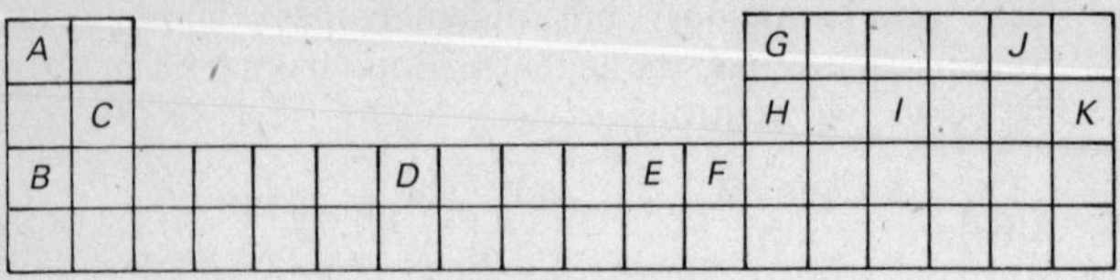

Figure 28

(b) (i) Select an element that can form ionic compounds where the element may be present in either the anion or the cation of the compound.

(ii) Write the formulae for two such ions. 2 *marks*

(c) (i) Select the element having the lowest boiling point.

(ii) How do you account for this low boiling point?
2 *marks*

(d) (i) Select an element which can form a molecular chloride whose molecule is planar.

(ii) Sketch the structure of this molecule, indicating its shape. 3 *marks*

(e) (i) Select an element which forms an amphoteric oxide.

(ii) Write the formula of this oxide. 1 *mark*

(f) (i) Select the element that could be the central ion of a colourless complex ion.

(ii) Write the formula of the complex ion, and draw a diagram to indicate its probable shape.
2 *marks*

(g) (i) Select an element which forms a compound which, on electrolysis, gives hydrogen at the anode.

(ii) Under what conditions would this take place?
2 *marks*
(L)

Answer

Note: In this type of question, on occasions, there may be more than one correct answer—only *one* of the possible correct answers is required. You are *not* expected to identify the element.

(a) (i) *D* (or *E* or *I*) can form compounds in which it can exhibit more than one oxidation state.

(ii) Oxides formed are DO, DO_2 (E_2O, EO; I_4O_6, I_4O_{10}) (Variable oxidation state is a characteristic of *d* block elements and of some *p* block elements).

(b) (i) *D* (or *E* or *F* or *H*) can form ionic compounds where the element is present in either the anion or cation.

(ii) Anion: KDO_4, K_2DO_4[$K_3E(CN)_6$; $Na_2F(OH)_4$; Na_3HF_6]

Cations: DCl_2[ESO_4; $F(NO_3)_2$; $H(SO_4)_3$]

(c) (i) *K* has the lowest boiling point (a noble gas).

(ii) *K* is a noble gas, existing as monatomic molecules that can only be attracted to each other by weak Van der Waals forces.

(d) (i) *G* forms a chloride with a planar molecule.

(ii)

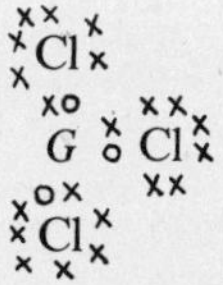

(e) (i) *H* (or *F*) forms an amphoteric oxide.

(ii) The formula is H_2O_3 (or FO).

(f) (i) *F* (or *H*) could be the central ion of a colourless complex.

(ii) $[F^{2+}(NH_3)_4]^{2+}$ or $[H^{3+}(OH^-)_4]^-$

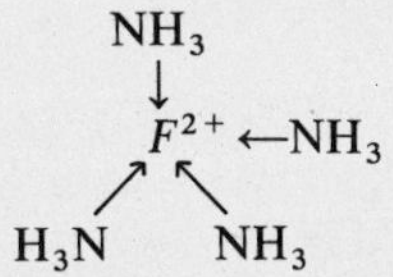

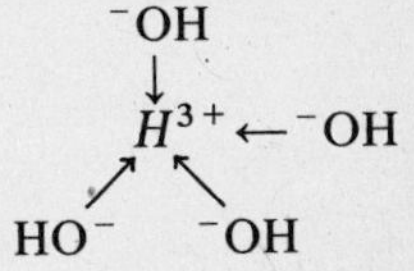

(g) (i) *B* (or *A*) (ionic hydrides containing the anion H give hydrogen at the anode).

(ii) Electrolysis of the molten hydride.

Example 5

The table gives some information about eight elements *A* to *H*, with consecutive atomic numbers; these letters are not the usual chemical symbols for the elements.

Element	Configuration of outer electrons	First ionization energy/ $kJ\,mol^{-1}$	Formula of typical oxide	Formula of typical chloride
A	$3s^2 3p^1$	580		
B		790		
C		1010		
D		1000		
E		1260		
F		1520		
G		420		
H	$3s^2 3p^6 4s^2$	590		

(a) Fill in the blank spaces in the table where appropriate. 6 *marks*

(b) Select from the elements *A* to *H*:

(i) a noble gas.
(ii) an alkaline earth metal.
(iii) a Group IV element. 3 *marks*

(c) Select from the elements *A* to *H*:

(i) one element which forms a basic oxide.
(ii) one which has an acidic oxide.
(iii) one which might form an amphoteric oxide.

3 *marks*

(L)

Answer

Element	Configuration of outer electrons	First ionization energy/ kJ mol^{-1}	Formula of typical oxide	Formula of typical chloride
A	$3s^2 3p^1$	580	A_2O_3	ACl_3
B	$3s^2 3p^2$	790	BO_2	BCl_4
C	$3s^2 3p^3$	1010	C_2O_5 (or C_2O_3)	CCl_5 (or CCl_3)
D	$3s^2 3p^4$	1000	DO_2 (or DO_3)	D_2Cl_2
E	$3s^2 3p^5$	1260	D_2O	DCl (or D_2)
F	$3s^2 3p^6$	1520	—	—
G	$3s^2 3p^6 4s^1$	420	G_2O	GCl
H	$3s^2 3p^6 4s^2$	590	HO	HCl_2

(b) (i) *F* is a noble gas.

(ii) *H* is an alkaline earth metal.

(iii) *B* is a Group IV element.

(c) (i) *G* (or *H*) forms a basic oxide.

(ii) *B* (or *C* or *D* or *E*) forms an acidic oxide.

(iii) *A* forms an amphoteric oxide.

Example 6

The table shows the atomic and ionic radii of the alkaline earth elements.

Element	Atomic radius /nm	Ionic radius /nm
Beryllium	0.112	0.030
Magnesium	0.160	0.065
Calcium	0.197	0.094
Strontium	0.215	0.110
Barium	0.221	0.134

(a) Using magnesium as an example, explain carefully what is meant by:

(i) atomic radius.

(ii) ionic radius. *4 marks*

(b) The ionic radius is, in each case, smaller than the atomic radius. Explain why this is so. *2 marks*

(c) Explain why the atomic radius increases from Be to Ba. *1 mark*

(d) The ions K^+ and Ca^{2+} have identical electronic configurations, yet the ionic radius of K^+ is larger than that of Ca^{2+}. Suggest why it is larger. *1 mark*

(e) Describe how you would prepare good specimens of:

(i) magnesium sulphate, $MgSO_4 . 7H_2O$, from magnesite (ie, native magnesium carbonate which may contain some calcium carbonate impurity).

(ii) barium sulphate, $BaSO_4$, from a sample of barium carbonate. *6 marks*

(L)

Answer

(a) **(i)** Atomic radius is half the distance between two atoms of magnesium in the metal lattice. This means that the centres of 2 atoms of magnesium are 0.320 nm apart.

(ii) Ionic radius is a measure of the space occupied by an ion in an ionic lattice. In the lattice of an ionic magnesium salt, the space occupied by each magnesium ion is 0.130 nm diameter.

(b) These elements form ions by loss of two electrons from the outer valency shell. The remaining electrons, from the penultimate shell inwards, are attracted by the protons from the nucleus with positive charges exceeding negative charges by two.

(c) Beryllium only has two shells of electrons whereas barium, in the sixth period, has a total of six shells of electrons.

(d) Although both ions have the same number of electrons, these are attracted by 19 protons in potassium but by 20 protons in calcium. This results in the electrons being attracted more by the calcium nucleus, hence the smaller ionic radius.

(e) **(i)** Magnesium sulphate could be obtained from magnesite by addition of excess dil sulphuric acid, to dissolve the magnesium carbonate. The calcium carbonate impurity would form insoluble calcium sulphate which could be filtered off, the filtrate then being concentrated by partial evaporation to crystallization point, then being left to cool and crystallize.

(ii) Barium carbonate would be dissolved in dil hydrochloric acid, warming to assist solution. Addition of dil sulphuric acid to the resultant solution after filtration would precipitate barium sulphate. This would be removed by filtration, the residue being washed with distilled water to remove impurities and then dried at just over 100°C.

Example 7

Iodine dissolves in hot concentrated solutions of sodium hydroxide according to the equation:

$$3I_2(s) + 6NaOH(aq) \rightarrow NaIO_3(aq) + 5NaI(aq) + 3H_2O(l)$$

In one experiment, 3.81 g of iodine were dissolved in 4 M sodium hydroxide solution.

(Relative atomic masses: H = 1; O = 16; Na = 23; I = 127.)

(a) (i) How many moles of iodine were used?

(ii) What volume of 4 M sodium hydroxide solution would be just sufficient to react with the iodine?

3 *marks*

(b) What reagent(s) would you add to solid sodium iodide to produce pure hydrogen iodide gas? 1 *mark*

(c) Iodine also reacts with aqueous sodium thiosulphate solution producing sodium iodide solution.

(i) Write a balanced equation, with state symbols, for the reaction.

(ii) Suggest a procedure by which solid sodium iodide might be obtained from the reaction mixture. 3 *marks*

(NUFF)

Answer

(a) (i) Moles of iodine $= \dfrac{3.81}{2 \times 127} = 0.015$ moles

(ii) From the equation: 3 moles ≡ 6 moles NaOH

∴ 0.015 moles ≡ 2 × 0.015 moles NaOH

4 moles NaOH are in 1 ℓ 4 M NaOH

0.03 moles NaOH are in $\dfrac{0.03}{4} \times 1000\,cm^3$ 4 M NaOH

$= 7.5\,cm^3$ 4 M NaOH

(b) Conc phosphoric acid might be added.

(c) (i) $I(s) + 2NaS_2O_3(aq) \rightarrow 2NaI(aq) + Na_2S_4O_6(aq)$

(ii) Sodium iodide might be obtained from the aqueous solution by fractional crystallization—concentrating the solution by partial evaporation then leaving to cool and crystallize. Depending on the relative solubilities of the two components the iodide would be either the major constituent of the crystals or of the filtrate.

Example 8

(a) (i) When 0.203 g of hydrated magnesium chloride, $MgCl_m . nH_2O$, were dissolved in water and titrated with 0.1 M silver nitrate ($AgNO_3$) solution, $20.0\,cm^3$ of the latter were required. A sample of the hydrated chloride lost 53.2% of its mass when heated in a stream of hydrogen chloride, leaving a residue of anhydrous magnesium chloride. From these figures calculate the values of *m* and *n*.

(ii) Is the value of *m*, calculated in (i), what you would have expected? Explain your answer.

6 marks

(b) When the hydrated chloride was heated in air instead of hydrogen chloride, the loss in mass was greater than 53.2% and both HCl and H_2O were evolved.

(i) What reaction do you think might have occurred and what was the solid product?

(ii) Why was a stream of hydrogen chloride used in (a)?

4 marks

(c) (i) What types of chemical bond exist in hydrated magnesium chloride? Indicate the particles involved in each type.

(ii) What is the type of bonding in sulphur dichloride, SCl_2?

(iii) Compare the physical properties of anhydrous magnesium chloride with those of sulphur dichloride, restricting your answer to two properties.

6 marks

(L)

Answer

(a) (i) 0.203 g contains $\frac{20}{1000} \times 0.1$ mol chlorine

$$\therefore \frac{0.203 \times 50}{1 \times 0.1} \text{ g } MgCl_m.nH_2O \text{ contains 1 mol chlorine}$$

$$= 101.5 \text{ g}$$

In 101.5 g $MgCl_m.nH_2O$ there are $\frac{53.2}{100} \times 101.5$ g water

$$= \frac{53.2}{100} \times \frac{101.5}{18} \text{ moles } H_2O$$

$= 3$ moles water (to nearest whole number).

In 101.5 g $MgCl_m.nH_2O$ there are 1 mol chlorine and 3 mols water

$$\frac{101.5-35.5-54}{24}=\frac{12}{24}\text{ mols}=\frac{1}{2}\text{ mol magnesium}$$

∴ 1 mol magnesium is combined with 2 mols chlorine and 6 mols water

$m=2$; $n=6$

(ii) Yes. Magnesium in Group II of the Periodic Table might be expected to have a valency of 2.

(b) (i) Hydrolysis of the chloride would explain this observation:

$$MgCl_2+H_2O \rightleftharpoons MgO+2HCl$$

The solid product was magnesium oxide.

(ii) To displace the above equilibrium to the left thus ensuring the magnesium chloride does not hydrolyse.

(c) (i) Ionic between magnesium ions and chloride ions; polar covalent between hydrogen atoms and oxygen atoms in water molecules.

(ii) The bonding is covalent.

(iii) Anhydrous magnesium chloride, being ionic, will be a solid with high melting point, due to the attraction between the oppositely charged ions. Sulphur dichloride will probably be a volatile liquid as it consists of discrete molecules with no significant attraction for each other. Magnesium chloride will be soluble in water, the sulphur dichloride will be insoluble in water—as it is a covalent chloride, it will hydrolyse rapidly.

Example 9

Black manganese(IV) oxide (manganese dioxide), *A*, was stirred into molten potassium hydroxide containing a suitable oxidizing agent. On cooling, the mixture was ground to break up the mass, boiled with water, and filtered. The filtrate was a green solution, *B*, which contained manganate(VI) ions. On acidifying solution *B*, the black powder *A* was formed in a hydrated condition and, on filtering, a purple solution *C* was left, which contained manganate(VII) (permanganate) ions. Solutions *B* and *C* can separately oxidize iron(II) to iron(III) in acid solution.

(a) Write the formula of anhydrous *A*. 2 *marks*

(b) Write the formula of *B*. 2 *marks*

(c) Balance the equation:

$A(s) + OH^-(aq) \longrightarrow B(aq) + H^+(aq) + e^-$ 3 *marks*

(*No other species are necessary*)

(d) Explain why (c) is an oxidation. 2 *marks*

(e) Balance the equation:

$3B(aq) + H^+(aq) \longrightarrow 1A(s) + 2C(aq) + H_2O$

(*No other species are necessary*) 3 *marks*

(f) Explain why (e) is an example of disproportionation. 4 *marks*

(g) Construct redox equations representing:

(i) the oxidation of $Fe^{2+}(aq)$, in acid solution, by *B*.

(ii) the oxidation of $Fe^{2+}(aq)$, in acid solution, by C.

In both cases *B* and *C* become Mn(II). 4 *marks*

(h) *Outlining* the essential practical details and the mode of calculation, show how the concentration (in $g\ell^{-1}$) of $FeSO_4.(NH_4)_2SO_4$ could be determined using reaction g(ii).

10 *marks*

(Relative atomic masses: H = 1; N = 14; O = 16; S = 32; Fe = 56.)

(SUJB)

Answer

(a) Manganese(IV) oxide has the formula MnO_2.

(b) *B* is potassium manganate(VI), K_2MnO_4.

(c) $MnO_2(s) + 2OH^-(aq) \rightarrow MnO_4^{2-}(aq) + 2H^+(aq) + 2e^-$

(d) Oxidation is a process of electron loss, which occurs in this case (alternatively: a substance is oxidized if its oxidation state is increased—in this case the oxidation state of manganese changes from +4 to +6, and hence oxidation has occurred).

(e) $3MnO_4^-(aq) + 4H^+(aq) \rightarrow MnO_2(s) + 2MnO_4^-(aq) + 2H_2O$

(f) Disproportionation occurs when a species reacts giving both an oxidation and a reduction product of itself. Here manganate(VI) is oxidized to manganate(VII) and reduced to manganese(IV) oxide.

(g) (i) $4Fe^{2+} + MnO_4^{2-} + 8H^+ \rightarrow 4Fe^{2+} + Mn^{2+} + 4H_2O$

(ii) $5Fe^{2+} + MnO_4^- + 8H^+ \rightarrow 5Fe^{3+} + Mn^{2+} + 4H_2O$

(h) A burette (0 to 50 cm^3) would be rinsed out, first with distilled water, then with a standard (0.02 M) potassium manganate solution, the washings being discarded. The burette would then be filled to the 0.00 cm^3 mark (or just below), making sure the jet below the tap was filled with solution. The actual burette reading would be noted (to nearest 0.05 cm^3).

A conical flask would be washed out with distilled water only, and a 25 cm^3 pipette washed with distilled water, then the iron(II) solution (a pipette bulb would be used with the pipette). Using the pipette, 25 cm^3 of the iron(II) solution would be transferred to the conical flask and an approximately equal volume of dilute sulphuric acid added to acidify the solution.

The manganate solution would then be added from the burette, shaking well to ensure mixing, if necessary rinsing the walls of the flask to wash splashes back into the main bulk of solution. The end point is when the solution just turns a permanent pink. The volume of manganate remaining in the burette is then recorded.

The titration is repeated until 2 consecutive concordant results (within 0.1 cm^3 of each other) are obtained.

If, in the above, the average titre is $a\,cm^3$, the concentration may be calculated:

From the equation (g) (ii) 1 mol $MnO_4^- \equiv 5$ mols Fe^{2+}

$$a\ cm^3 \text{ of } 0.02\,\text{M}\ MnO_4^- \text{ contains } \frac{a}{1000} \times 0.02 \text{ mol } MnO_4^-$$

$$\therefore\ 25\ cm^3 \text{ of } Fe^{2+} \text{ solution contains } \frac{5a \times 0.02}{1000} \text{ mol } Fe^{2+}$$

1 ℓ of Fe^{2+} solution contains

$$\frac{5a \times 0.02}{1000} \times \frac{1000}{25} \text{ mols } Fe^{2+} = 0.004a \text{ mols } Fe^{2+}.$$

$Mr[FeSO_4.(NH_4)_2SO_4]$

$$= 56 + (32 + 64) + 2 \times 18 + (32 + 64) = 284$$

$\therefore$ Concentration of $FeSO_4.(NH_4)_2SO_4$

$$= 0.004a \times 284\ g\,\ell^{-1}$$

$$= 1.136\,a\ g\,\ell^{-1}$$

Chapter 7

s, p and *d* block

Example 1

Group VI of the Periodic Table contains the elements oxygen, sulphur, selenium, tellurium, and polonium in increasing order of atomic number. The most common oxidation numbers in this group of elements are −2, +4 and +6.

(a) Write the formula of a hydride of sulphur in the −2 oxidation state. *2 marks*

(b) Write the formula of an oxide of selenium in the +4 oxidation state. *2 marks*

(c) Write the formula of an oxoacid of tellurium in the +6 oxidation state. *2 marks*

(d) Which of these elements is likely to be radioactive? *1 mark*

(e) Write an equation representing the thermal decomposition of the compound in (a). *2 marks*

(f) Put the hydrides of this Group in order of increasing stability to heat. *2 marks*

(g) Using iron(II) sulphide and dil sulphuric acid as reagents, and a tap funnel, conical flask, delivery tube and Bunsen burner as apparatus, draw a diagram to show how you would demonstrate the thermal decomposition of hydrogen sulphide. *4 marks*

Say how you would identify the products. *2 marks*

(h) Place the oxides of sulphur, selenium and tellurium (all in the +4 oxidation state) in order of increasing acidity. *2 marks*

Give some explanation of the order listed. 2 *marks*

(i) The equation:

$$H_2SeO_4(aq) + 2OH^-(aq) = 2H_2O(l) + SeO_4^{2-}(aq)$$

represents the reaction of selenic(VI) acid with hydroxyl (hydroxide) ions.

(i) Which species in this equation is donating protons? 1 *mark*

(ii) Which species in this equation is accepting protons? 1 *mark*

(iii) Explain why this reaction is regarded as a neutralization. 2 *marks*

(j) Suggest a theoretical interpretation for the lesser volatility of water when compared with hydrogen sulphide. 2 *marks*

(k) Indicate how sodium thiosulphate is used in photography and in volumetric analysis.

3 *marks*
(SUJB)

Answer

(a) H_2S.

(b) SeO_2.

(c) H_2TeO_4.

(d) Polonium.

(e) $H_2S \rightleftharpoons H_2 + S$.

(f) $H_2Po < H_2Te < H_2Se < H_2S < H_2O$
Least stable Most stable

(g) See Figure 29. The sulphur would appear as a mobile amber liquid on the walls of the glass delivery tube. Hydrogen would burn with a squeaky pop.

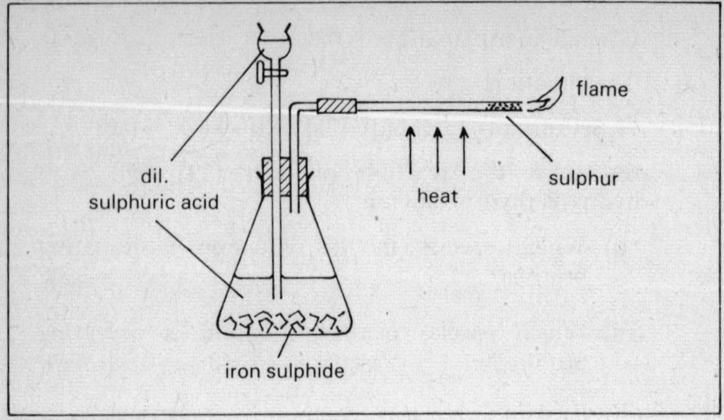

Figure 29

(h) $TeO_2 < SeO_2 < SO_2$
Most acidic

On ascending a group the elements become less metallic and hence the oxides more acidic.

(i) (i) H_2SeO_4.
(ii) OH^-.
(iii) One species donates protons to the other, forming water.

(j) Water is extensively hydrogen bonded, whereas hydrogen sulphide is not.

(k) In photography it removes unchanged silver bromide as a complex ion. In volumetric analysis it acts as a reducing agent, in particular for estimating iodine.

Example 2

This question concerns the *d* block elements from Sc ($Z=21$) to Zn ($Z=30$).

(a) In the spaces, insert the electronic configurations of the ions shown.

	3d					4s
Sc^{3+} (Ar)						
Mn^{3+} (Ar)						
Zn^{2+} (Ar)						

Which of these ions (if any) are colourless?

What feature of electronic configuration is responsible for the lack of colour in some ions of *d* block elements?
5 *marks*

(b) (i) Give the formula of a compound or ion containing manganese in the +7 oxidation state.

(ii) Explain in terms of electronic configuration how the +7 oxidation state arises.

(iii) What is the maximum possible oxidation state of vanadium ($Z = 23$)?
4 *marks*

(c) (i) How would you obtain an aqueous solution of the complex ion $[Cr(NH_3)_6]^{3+}$?

(ii) What is the oxidation state of chromium in this ion?

(iii) Give the stereo-structure of the ion,

(iv) Give the name of the ion, $[Cr(NH_3)_4Cl_2]^-$, and draw the stereo-structures of two isomers of it.
6 *marks*
(L)

Answer

(a)

	3d					4s
Sc^{3+} (Ar)						
Mn^{3+} (Ar)	↑		↑	↑		
Zn^{2+} (Ar)	↑↓	↑↓	↑↓	↑↓	↑↓	

Zn^{2+} and Sc^{3+} are colourless.

Ions with an unfilled or fully filled *d* shell are colourless.

(b) **(i)** $KMnO_4$.

(ii) The seven outer electrons of manganese are shared with the four oxygen atoms.

(iii) +5.

(c) **(i)** By adding aqueous ammonia in excess to an aqueous solution of a chromium(III) compound.

(ii) +3.

(iii)

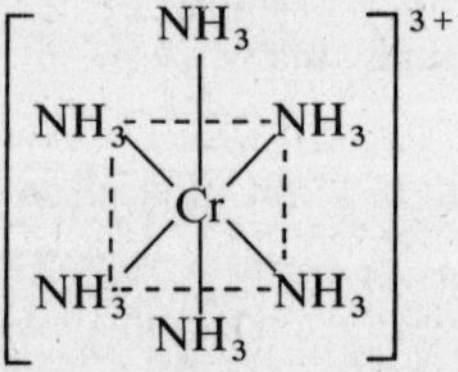

octahedral

(iv) Tetraamminedichlorochromium(III).

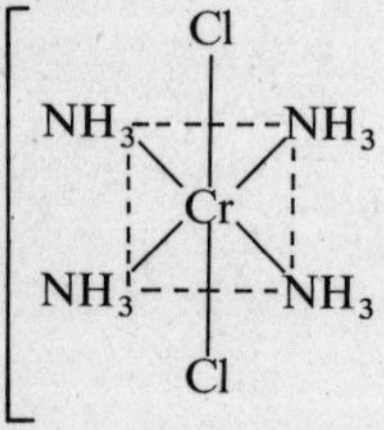

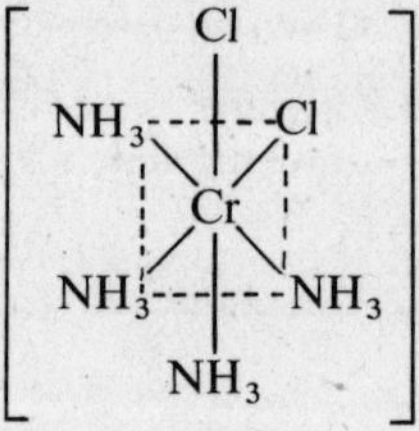

Example 3

(a) State how the following properties of the elements in Group VII of the Periodic Table vary with increasing atomic number:

(i) atomic radius.

(ii) electronegativity.

(iii) first ionization energy.

(iv) the reducing power of the hydrides. 4 *marks*

(b) A sodium halide reacts with cold concentrated sulphuric acid to give *colourless* fumes. On warming the mixture *brown* fumes are obtained.

(i) Name the halide ion in the salt.

(ii) Write the equation for the reaction which gives colourless fumes.

(iii) Write the equation for the reaction which gives brown fumes, and state why the brown fumes are formed. 6 *marks*

(AEB: Nov 1980)

Answer

(a) **(i)** Increases.

(ii) Decreases.

(iii) Decreases.

(iv) Increases.

(b) **(i)** Bromide.

(ii) $NaBr + H_2SO_4 \rightarrow NaHSO_4 + HBr$

(iii) $2HBr + H_2SO_4 \rightarrow SO_2 + 2H_2O + Br_2$

Bromide ions are oxidized to bromine by sulphuric acid.

Example 4

This question concerns complex ions of the transition elements.

(a) (i) Choose ONE complex anion of copper and ONE complex cation of silver and complete the following table to show the formula and the oxidation number of the transition metal in each case.

	Formula	Oxidation number of metal
Complex anion of copper		
Complex cation of silver		

(ii) Describe the bonding between the metal and the ligands in ONE of these complex ions.

5 *marks*

(b) Nickel forms a complex ion $[Ni(NH_3)_6]^{2+}$. Show in a diagram the probable shape of this ion. 1 *mark*

(c) Nickel forms a complex with the hexadentate ligand, EDTA, which has the formula:

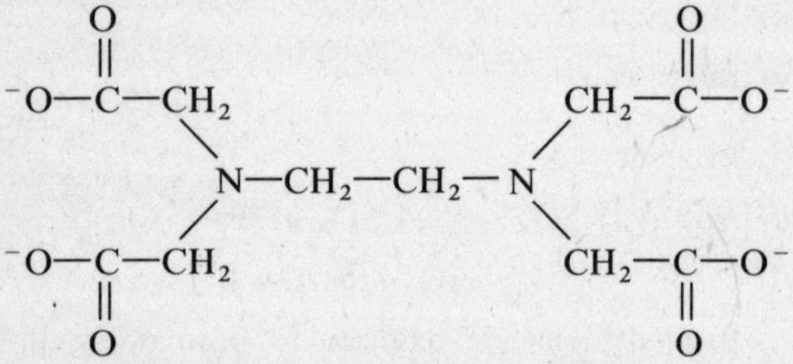

(i) What is meant by the term *hexadentate*?

(ii) On the formula above, indicate by asterisks (*) the points of bonding with the metal. 2 *marks*

(d) (i) Write an expression for the stability constant of the tetramminecopper(II) ion, $[Cu(NH_3)_4]^{2+}$.

(ii) When aqueous sodium hydroxide is added to a solution of this complex in water, a small quantity of copper(II) hydroxide is formed, but when hydrogen sulphide gas is passed through such a solution almost all the copper is precipitated as copper(II) sulphide. Suggest an explanation for this difference in behaviour.

4 *marks*

(L)

Answer

(a) **(i)**

Formula	Oxidation number of metal
$[CuCl_2]^-$	+1
$[Ag(NH_3)_2]^+$	+1

(ii) Dative covalent. The ammonia lone pair is donated to a vacant silver orbital.

(b)

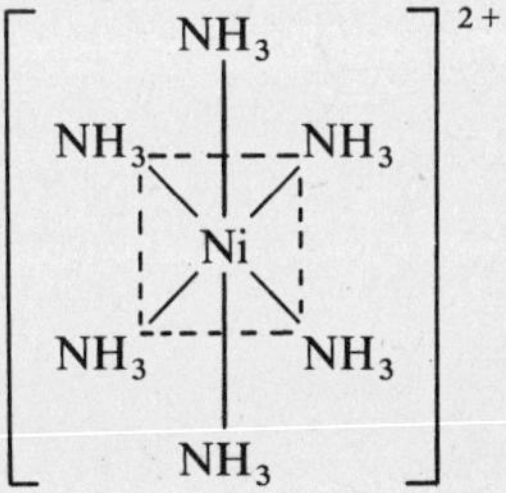

octahedral

(c) **(i)** Six binding sites.

(ii)

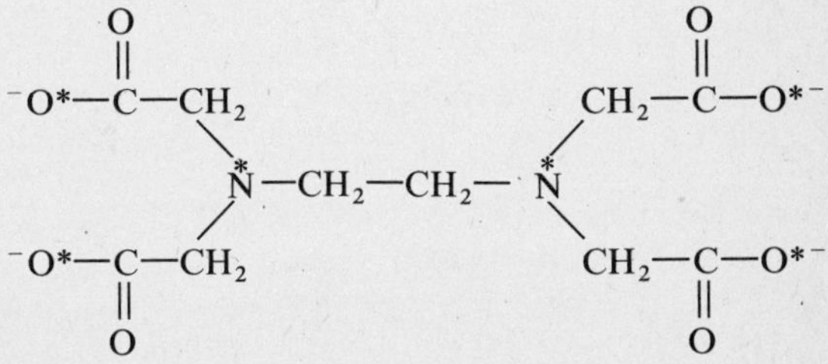

(d) **(i)** $$K=\frac{[[Cu(NH_3)_4]^{2+}]}{[Cu(aq)^{2+}][NH_3(aq)]^4}$$

(ii) Hydrogen sulphide will react with aqueous ammonia to form ammonium ions. The concentration of aqueous ammonia is lowered and more Cu^{2+}(aq) ions are formed in the equilibrium and CuS_2 is precipitated. Hydroxide ion maintains the high concentration of aqueous ammonia.

Example 5

The element gallium (symbol Ga) occurs in Group III of the Periodic Table, one row below aluminium and one row above the element indium. The existence of gallium was predicted by Mendeleev a few years before its discovery in 1875. Gallium has similar properties to aluminium, reacting with potassium hydroxide releasing hydrogen, forming an amphoteric hydroxide and burning in chlorine to form a chloride.

(a) The value accepted in 1870 for the relative atomic mass of aluminium was 27 and that for indium was 113. Suggest, giving your reasons, a value for the relative atomic mass of gallium.

2 *marks*

(b) (i) What oxidation number would you expect gallium to have in its compounds?

(ii) Deduce a formula for gallium hydroxide.

(iii) What would be the product(s) of the reaction of gallium hydroxide with dilute aqueous nitric acid?

(iv) What would be the product(s) of the reaction of gallium hydroxide with dilute aqueous sodium hydroxide?

5 *marks*

(c) Suggest an experimental procedure by which gallium potassium sulphate, 'gallium alum', might be prepared from gallium metal.

3 *marks*

(d) (i) Gallium forms a chloride if the element is heated in a stream of chlorine gas. The chloride is a white solid melting at 78°C and boiling at 202°C. Complete Figure 30 to show how a sample of gallium chloride might be collected.

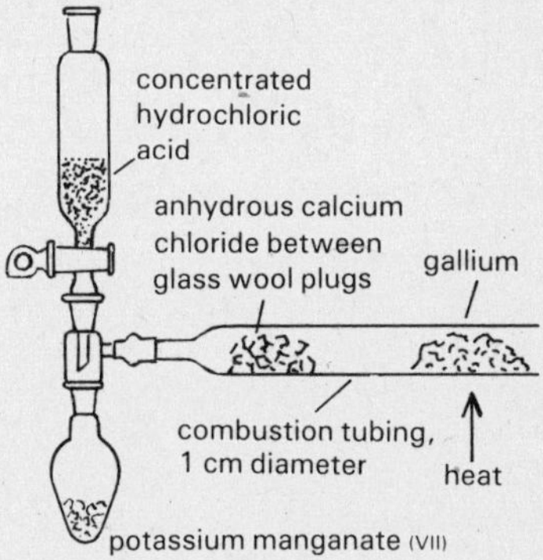

Figure 30

(ii) What is the purpose of the anhydrous calcium chloride in the apparatus?

3 *marks*

(e) A sample of gallium chloride weighing 0.1 g was vaporized and it was found to occupy 16 cm^3 at a temperature of 415°C and at a pressure of 1 atm.

(i) Calculate a value for the relative formula mass of gallium chloride under the conditions of the experiment. (Molar volume of a gas at 0°C and 1 atm $= 22.4\,\ell\,mol^{-1}$ or $R = 0.082\,atm\,\ell\,K^{-1}\,mol^{-1}$.)

(ii) Suggest a molecular formula for gallium chloride in the vapour state, indicating how you arrive at your answer. (Relative atomic mass: Cl $= 35.5$.)

4 *marks*
(NUFF)

Answer

(a) 70. This is the average of the relative molecular mass for aluminium and indium.

(b) (i) Three.

(ii) $Ga(OH)_3$.

(iii) $Ga(NO_3)_3 + 3H_2O$.

(iv) $Na[Ga(OH)_4]$.

(c) Pieces of metallic gallium are added to a solution of potassium hydroxide so that the gallium and potassium are in approximately equimolar proportions. A slight excess of sulphuric acid is added carefully. The mixture is boiled, filtered and allowed to cool, when crystals will slowly form.

(d) (i) See Figure 30.

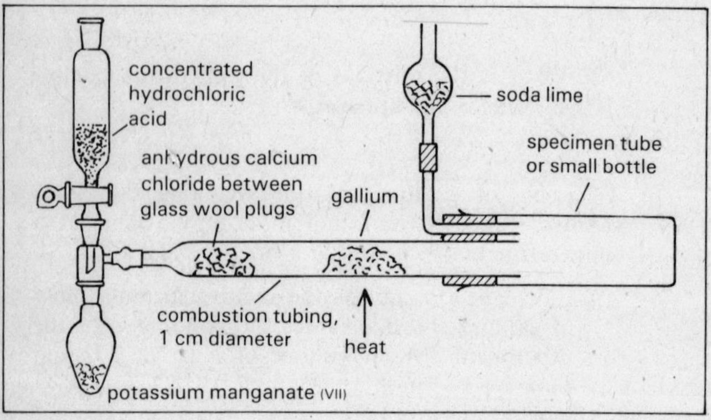

Figure 31

(ii) To prevent water vapour entering the reaction chamber.

(e) (i) 0.1 g $GaCl_3$ occupies 16 cm^3 at 415°C and 1 atm pressure.

$$0.1\,g\,GaCl_3 \text{ occupies } \frac{16\times 273}{688}\,cm^3 \text{ at stp}$$

$$\frac{0.1\times 688\times 2240}{16\times 273}\,GaCl_3 \text{ occupies } 22.4\,\ell \text{ at stp}$$

$\therefore$ Relative molecular mass is 353.

(ii) $Mr(GaCl_3) = 70 + 3\times 35.5 = 176.5$

Molecular formula is Ga_2Cl_6(Mr353).

Example 6

This question is about interhalogen compounds that are compounds of two or more halogen elements only. Examples are ClF, ClF_3, ICl, BrF, BrCl, BrF_5 and IF_7. Several others are known. Like the halogens themselves, interhalogen compounds are usually quite reactive.

(a) Draw diagrams to show the electronic structure ('dot and cross' diagrams) of the following interhalogens (only the outer-shell electrons need be shown):

(i) iodine monochloride, ICl.

(ii) bromine pentafluoride, BrF_5. 3 *marks*

(b) Draw a diagram to show the shape you would expect for a molecule of bromine pentafluoride, BrF_5.

2 *marks*

(c) Most of the interhalogen compounds known are fluorides. Suggest a reason for this.

2 *marks*

(d) Benzene undergoes a substitution reaction with chlorine according to the following equation:

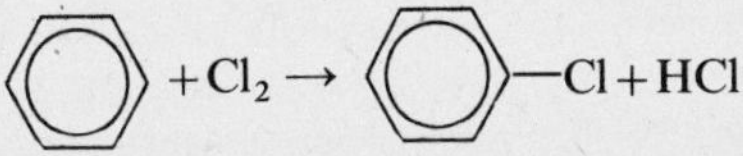

This reaction occurs only in the presence of a substance such as iron filings. Iodine does not react directly with benzene under these conditions.

In contrast, benzene readily undergoes a substitution reaction with the interhalogen, iodine monochloride, ICl.

(i) Suggest a reason for the ready reaction of iodine monochloride with benzene.

(ii) Write an equation for the reaction of benzene with iodine monochloride.

4 *marks*

(NUFF)

Answer

(a) (i)

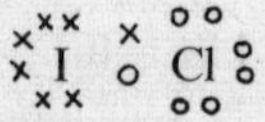

(ii)

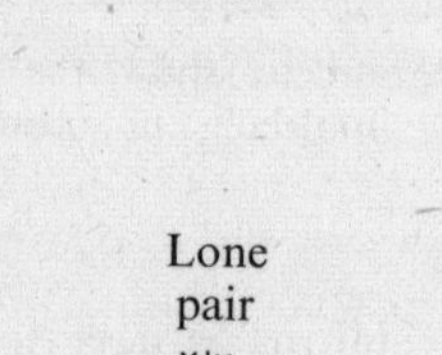

(b)

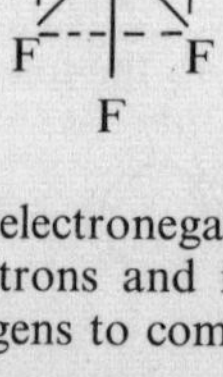

(c) Fluorine is the most electronegative element. It has a very great affinity for electrons and is therefore most likely to encourage other halogens to combine with it.

(d) (i) ICl is polarized $\overset{\delta^-}{\mathrm{Cl}}\text{—}\overset{\delta^+}{\mathrm{I}}$. When it undergoes an electrophilic substitution reaction with benzene, the delocalized electrons can readily attack the positive iodine atom.

(ii) 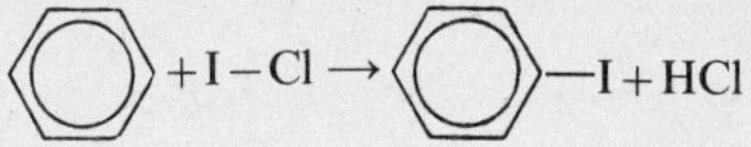

Example 7

This question concerns the elements of Group IV of the Periodic Table: carbon, silicon, germanium, tin and lead.

(a) (i) What is the electron structure in the outer shell of the atoms of each element?

(ii) The tetrachlorides of these elements have the same molecular shape. What is this shape, and what is the nature of the bonding present in the molecules?

(iii) Silicon tetrachloride reacts vigorously with water. Give an equation for this reaction.

Unlike silicon tetrachloride, carbon tetrachloride does not react with water. Explain this difference in behaviour. 6 *marks*

(b) Give the structure of:

(i) carbon dioxide.

(ii) silicon dioxide.

Although the carbon–oxygen bond is polar, carbon dioxide does not have a dipole moment. How do you account for this? 4 *marks*

(c) (i) Tin(II) compounds show reducing properties. Give ONE example of this behaviour, and write an equation for the reaction.

(ii) Lead(IV) oxide has oxidizing properties. Describe ONE example of this behaviour, and write an equation for the reaction. 4 *marks*

(L)

(d) When dil hydrochloric acid is added to a solution of lead(II) nitrate, a white precipitate is formed; but, if conc acid is used, much less precipitate is formed.

(i) What is the white solid formed?

Write an ionic equation for the reaction.

(ii) Explain this difference in behaviour.

4 *marks*

(L)

Answer

(a) **(i)** s^2p^2.

(ii) The tetrachlorides are tetrahedral: the bonding is covalent.

(iii) $SiCl_4 + 3H_2O \rightarrow H_2SiO_3 + 3HCl$

It is believed that the reaction proceeds by the water molecule donating an oxygen lone pair to a vacant *d* orbital of silicon. Carbon being a first-row element does not have any available *d* orbitals.

(b) **(i)** O=C=O

(ii)

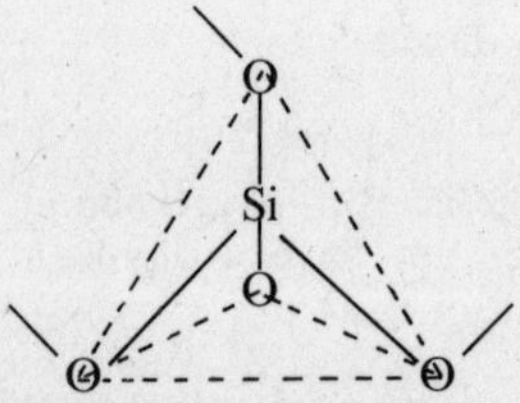

Carbon dioxide is non-polar because it is a symmetrically linear molecule. The double bonds are oppositely polarized and any effect is cancelled out.

(c) **(i)** Tin(II) compounds can reduce iron(III) to iron(II):

$2Fe^{3+} + Sn^{2+} \rightarrow 2Fe^{2+} + Sn^{4+}$

(ii) Lead(IV) oxide liberates chlorine from conc hydrochloric acid:

$$PbO_2 + 4HCl \rightarrow PbCl_2 + 2H_2O + Cl_2$$

(d) (i) Lead(II) chloride:

$$Pb^{2+} + 2Cl^- \rightarrow PbCl_2$$

(ii) With conc acid a complex ion is formed:

$$Pb^{2+} + 4Cl^- \rightleftharpoons PbCl_4^{2-}$$

$Pb[PbCl_4]$ is soluble and reduces the amount of precipitated $PbCl_2$.

Chapter 8
Organic chemistry

Example 1

(a) For each of parts (i) to (viii) ONE or MORE of the alternatives *A*, *B*, *C* and *D* listed below are correct. Decide which of the alternatives is (are) correct and write the appropriate letter(s) in answer to the question.

A $CH_3.CH_2.C{\equiv}C.CH_3$

B $CH_3.CH{=}CH.CH{=}CH_2$

C $CH_3.CH_2.CH_2.C{\equiv}CH$

D 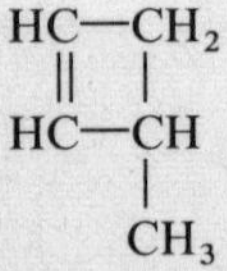

(i) Which will decolorize bromine water?

(ii) Which will yield methanal (formaldehyde) on ozonolysis and hydrolysis of the product?

(iii) Which will be converted to pentane by catalytic hydrogenation?

(iv) Which will give a compound of empirical formula CH_2 on complete hydrogenation?

(v) Which will give a pale yellow precipitate with an aqueous solution containing diamminosilver(I) ions $[Ag(NH_3)_2]^+(aq)$?

(vi) Which will have four carbon atoms arranged linearly?

(vii) Which will contain the shortest carbon to carbon bonds?

(viii) Which will have a systematic name ending in -yne?

15 *marks*

(b) A hydrocarbon, *E* (C_4H_6) gives a red precipitate, *F*, with a solution of copper(I) chloride in aqueous ammonia. *E* also reacts with water in the presence of sulphuric acid and mercury(II) sulphate, forming compound *G*.

G was unaffected by neutral potassium manganate(VII) (potassium permanganate), but it reacted with iodine in warm aqueous sodium hydroxide to give a yellow crystalline precipitate, *H*, with a characteristic odour.

Deduce the structural formulae of *E*, *F*, *G* and *H*, and explain the above reactions. 15 *marks*

(SUJB)

Answer

(a) **(i)** *A*, *B*, *C* and *D* will decolorize bromine water (they are all unsaturated).

(ii) *B* will yield methanal on ozonolysis (the terminal double bond is split, the $=CH_2$ unit giving the product methanal).

(iii) *A*, *B* and *C* give pentane on hydrogenation (*D* does not as it has a cyclic structure).

(iv) *D* gives C_5H_{10} (empirical formula CH_2) on complete hydrogenation (due to its cyclic structure).

(v) *C* gives a pale yellow precipitate with this reagent (it contains a terminal $-C{\equiv}C-H$, the attached hydrogen having acidic character).

(vi) *A* has four carbon atoms arranged linearly (the bonding of the $-C{\equiv}C-$ involves *sp* hybridization giving a linear arrangement to the atoms joined either side of the bond).

(vii) *A* and *C* have the shortest carbon-to-carbon bonds ($C{\equiv}C$ bonds are shorter than $C{=}C$).

(viii) *A* and *C* have systematic names ending -yne (the name characteristic for a compound containing a $-C{\equiv}C-$ bond.

(b) Structural formulae are:

E

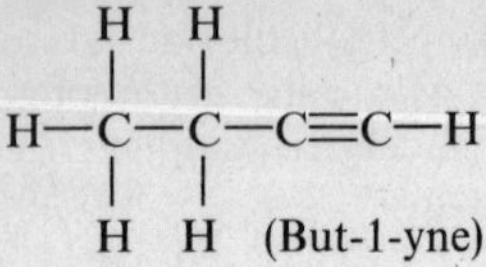

(But-1-yne)

F

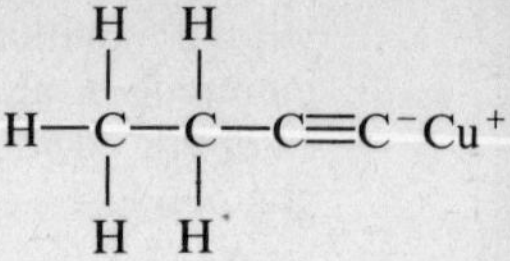

G

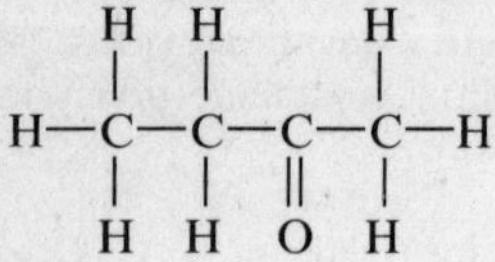

(Butan-2-one)

H

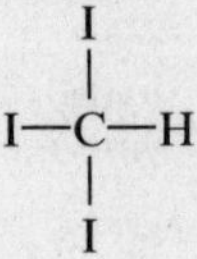

(Triodomethane)

Explanation: E must contain a terminal $—C{\equiv}C—H$ bond to give an insoluble copper(I) derivative.

G is formed from *E* by addition of H_2O.

This addition obeys Markownikow's rule resulting in a ketone. Ketones are not oxidized by potassium manganate(VII).

G contains a $CH_3—\underset{|}{C}{=}O$ unit.

All compounds containing this grouping react with iodine and alkali, by a reaction involving both substitution and oxidation to give triiodomethane.

Example 2

(a) Write the structural formulae of (i) butan-2-ol, (ii) a structural isomer of butan-2-ol. 2 *marks*

(b) Butan-2-ol exists in two isomeric forms. Write structural formulae to show the difference in the arrangement of atoms in space in the two isomers and *name* the type of isomerism exhibited by them. 3 *marks*

(c) (i) Write the structural formulae of an aldehyde containing four carbon atoms, and of a ketone containing four carbon atoms.

(ii) Give one test which you would use to distinguish between this aldehyde and ketone, indicating name of reagent, conditions and result.
5 marks
(AEB: Nov 1980)

Answer

(a) (i) $CH_3.CH_2CH(OH).CH_3$

(ii) $CH_3.CH_2.CH_2.CH_2.OH$

(b)

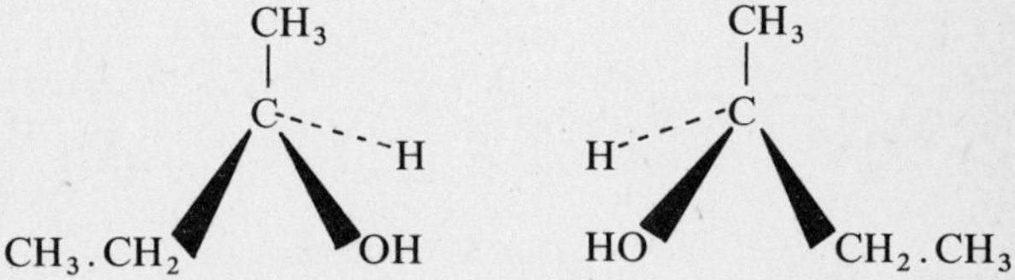

Type of isomerism: optical

(c) (i)

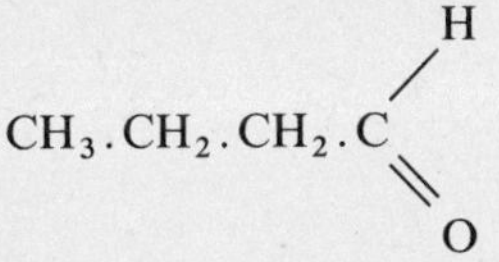

is an aldehyde with 4 carbon atoms.

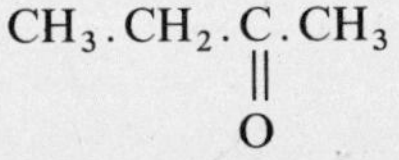

is a ketone.

(ii) *Reagent*: acidified potassium dichromate(VI).
Conditions: warm mixture gently.
Result: the aldehyde turns the dichromate(VI) green by reducing it. There is no reaction with the ketone.

Example 3

Each of the following pieces of information could apply to one or more compounds. In each case give the name and structure of *one* compound to which the information could apply. Explain your reasoning and, as far as possible, write equations for the reactions involved.

A is a liquid that reacts slowly with concentrated aqueous sodium hydroxide. Addition of water results in the formation of two immiscible liquids, one of which is an aqueous solution. The aqueous solution, on addition of conc hydrochloric acid precipitates a white solid that effervesces when aqueous sodium carbonate is added.

B is a liquid, that on treatment with concentrated ammonia, reacts vigorously forming a solid. The solid, on treatment with aqueous sodium hydroxide and bromine, produces a liquid with fairly strong basic properties.

C is a liquid which, on treatment with an ice-cold mixture of sodium nitrite and dil sulphuric acid, evolves a colourless gas and produces a liquid. The liquid gives a yellow crystalline solid on treatment with aqueous sodium hydroxide and iodine.

D is a liquid. One molecule of *D* contains two atoms of chlorine, one of which is much more readily removed than the other on treatment with aqueous sodium hydroxide.

E is a solid that on heating produces a liquid in poor yield, and a solid. The liquid forms a crystalline 2,4-dinitrophenylhydrazone, and the solid effervesces on addition of dil hydrochloric acid. (L)

Answer

Substances that might react as indicated are:

A benzyl benzoate, $C_6H_5.COO.CH_2.C_6H_5$. This, on hydrolysis with alkali would give benzyl alcohol (phenylmethanol), a liquid immiscible with water, together with sodium benzoate, which is soluble in water. Acidification of its aqueous solution would give the insoluble benzoic acid as a white crystalline solid. As this is an acid, it would react with sodium carbonate to give carbon dioxide.

Equations:

$C_6H_5.COO.CH_2.C_6H_5 + NaOH \rightarrow$
$C_6H_5.COONa + C_6H_5.CH_2OH$

$C_6H_5.COONa(aq) + H^+(aq) \rightarrow C_6H_5.COOH(s) + Na^+(aq)$

$2C_6H_5.COOH + Na_2CO_3 \rightarrow 2C_6H_5.COONa + H_2O + CO_2$

(suitable alternatiyes include (i) benzaldehyde (benzene carbaldehyde) $C_6H_5.CHO$, which disproportionates with alkali to give products identical to above: (ii) esters of other aromatic carboxylic acids with aromatic or higher aliphatic alcohols.

B propanoyl chloride, $C_2H_5.COCl$, which reacts with conc ammonia to give propanamide. This, being an amide is a solid, which reacts with bromine and alkali to give an amine with one fewer carbon atom. Alkylamines are stronger bases than ammonia hence the product has fairly strong basic properties.

Equations:

$C_2H_5.COCl + 2NH_3 \rightarrow C_2H_5.CONH_2 + NH_4Cl$

$C_2H_5.CONH_2 + Br_2 + 4OH^- \rightarrow$
$C_2H_5NH_2 + 2Br^- + CO_3^{2-} + 2H_2O$

(suitable alternatives are alkyl acid chlorides other than ethanoyl chloride—this gives methylamine as the end product, which is a gas.)

C 2-propylamine, $CH_3.CH(NH_2).CH_3$. The reaction with sodium nitrite and dil acid indicates the presence of an NH_2 (amino) group. In this reaction the amino group is replaced by an —OH group and nitrogen is also given off. The alcohol produced must contain a $CH_3—\overset{|}{\underset{|}{C}}—O$ group as the second reaction is specific for this group, the yellow crystalline solid being triiodomethane.

Equations:

(i) $CH_3.CH(NH_2).CH_3 + NO_2^- + H^+ \rightarrow$
$CH_3.CH(OH).CH_3 + N_2 + H_2O$

(ii) (a) $CH_3.CH(OH).CH_3 + I_2 + 2NaOH \rightarrow$
$CH_3.CO.CH_3 + 2I^- + 2H_2O$

(b) $CH_3CO.CH_3 + 3I_2 \rightarrow CI_3.CO.CH_3 + 3HI$

(c) $CI_3COCH_3 + NaOH \rightarrow CHI_3 + CH_3.COONa$

(other compounds are any alkylamines with the group $CH_3.CH(NH_2).R$ including ethylamine and ethanamide—the latter is the only amide containing a $CH_3.C{=}O$ group).

D 4-chlorobenzylchloride [1-chloro-4-(chloromethyl)benzene] $ClCH_2.C_6H_4.Cl$ contains two chlorine atoms. The one attached to the alkyl group is hydrolysed by refluxing with aqueous alkali, but the atom attached directly to the aromatic nucleus is not so easily hydrolysed, having to be heated with the aqueous alkali under pressure. This is because attachment to the aromatic nucleus containing delocalized electrons, strengthens the bond making it more difficult to break the bond.

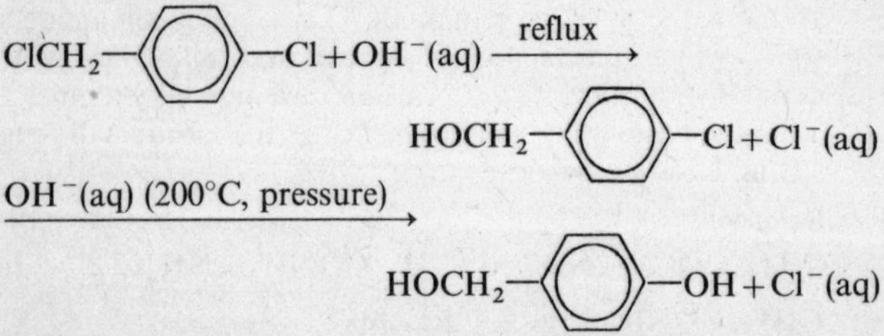

(Alternative substances include isomers of the above with the chlorine in the 2 or 3 positions and chloro-substituted acyl chlorides in which the acyl chloride group hydrolyses at room temperature.)

E Calcium salts of carboxylic acids [eg, calcium ethanoate, $Ca(OOC.CH_3)_2$] react to give products which behave as indicated. These decompose to give a ketone (except for the methanoate, which gives methanal and aldehyde). Ketones contain the carbonyl group, which condenses with 2,4-dinitrophenylhydrazine to give corresponding crystalline 2,4-dinitrophenylhydrazones. The other product of the decomposition is calcium carbonate, a solid which reacts with acids to give carbon dioxide, evolved with effervescence:

$$Ca(OOC.CH_3)_2 \xrightarrow{\text{heat}} CH_3.CO.CH_3 + CaCO_3$$

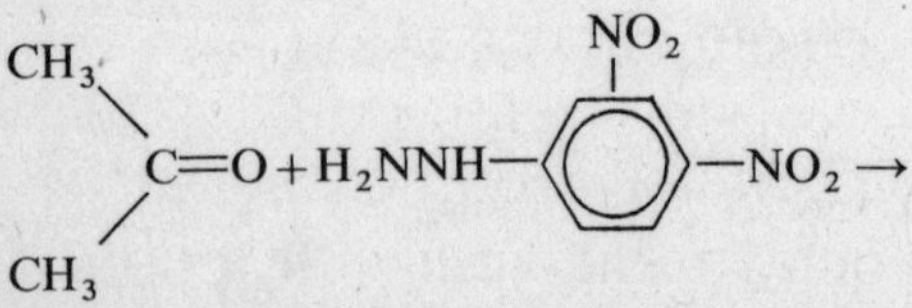

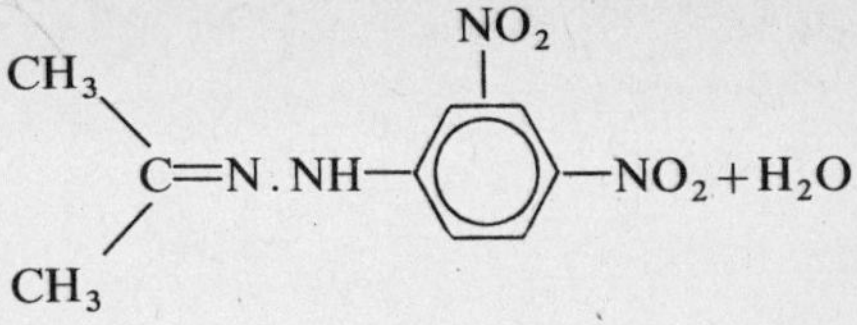

$$CaCO_3(s) + 2H^+(aq) \rightarrow Ca^{2+}(aq) + H_2O + CO_2$$

Example 4

(a) Give the systematic name for each of the following compounds:

A $CH_3.CH_2.CH_2NH_2$

B $CH_3.CH_2.CONH_2$

C $C_6H_5.NH_2$

D $CH_3.CH_2.COONH_4$ 2 *marks*

(b) (i) State which of these compounds will react with aqueous sodium hydroxide to form ammonia.

(ii) Write an equation for ONE such reaction.

2 *marks*

(c) State which of the compounds *A* to *C* shows the least basic character. Explain your choice. 2 *marks*

(d) Give the reagents and conditions which you would use to

(i) prepare *A* from *B*.

(ii) convert *B* into ethylamine. 4 *marks*

(e) (i) Give the reagents and conditions by which *C* may be converted into a diazonium salt, and hence into an azo dye.

(ii) Give the structure of the diazonium salt.

(iii) Explain why the diazonium salt obtained from *C* is relatively stable compared with the analogous diazonium salt which might be expected to form from *A*. 6 *marks*

(L)

Answer

(a) *A* is 1-propylamine.
B is propanamide
C is phenylamine.
D is ammonium propanoate.

(b) (i) *B* and *D* react with alkali to give ammonia.

(ii) $CH_3.CH_2.CONH_2 + OH^- \rightarrow$

$$CH_3.CH_2.COO^- + NH_3$$

(or $CH_3.CH_2.COONH_4 + OH^- \rightarrow$

$$CH_3.CH_2.COO^- + NH_3 + H_2O)$$

(c) *B* is the least basic due to the electron attracting nature of the oxygen in the >C=O bond. This reduces the electron density available on the nitrogen to attract protons.

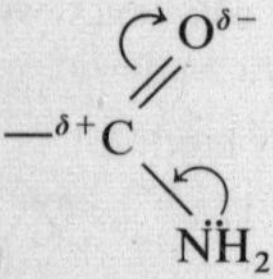

(d) (i) Reduce *B* by adding ethanol then sodium to the solid.

(ii) Add bromine and dilute alkali to *B*, then add conc alkali and warm the mixture.

(e) (i) Dissolve *C* in excess dil sulphuric (or hydrochloric) acid. Cool to below 5°C and add cooled aqueous sodium nitrite, keeping the temperature below 5°C. Finally add the product to phenol dissolved in dil sodium hydroxide.

(ii)

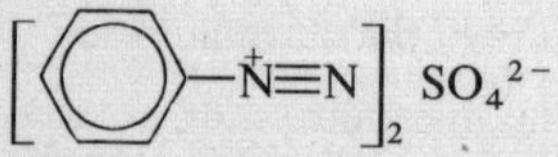

(iii) In the diazonium salt from *C* the aromatic nucleus contains delocalized electrons which stabilises the structure. There are no delocalized electrons in *A* as it is an aliphatic amine.

Example 5

The following is a route to the formation of 2,2-dimethylpropanoic acid, $C_5H_{10}O_2$.

A C_4H_8

$\downarrow$ Conc HBr

B ....

$\downarrow$ KCN/dil H_2SO_4

C C_5H_8N

$\downarrow$

D $C_5H_{10}O_2$

(a) *B* has the composition carbon 35.04%, hydrogen 6.57%, bromine 58.39%. Calculate the empirical formula of *B*. 3 *marks*

(b) Give the structures of *A*, *B*, *C* and *D*. 6 *marks*

(c) Give the reagents and conditions of reaction for the conversion of *C* into *D*. 2 *marks*

(d) A student who carried out the above sequence of reactions started with 5.6 ℓ of *A* at stp and obtained 8.5 g of *D*. Calculate the overall percentage yield of *D*. 3 *marks*

(e) Using a similar series of reactions, it is possible to obtain 2-methylbutanoic acid ($C_5H_{10}O_2$). Give the structures of the TWO hydrocarbons which could be used to produce this acid. 3 *marks*

(L)

Answer

(a) $$C{:}H{:}Br = \frac{35.04}{12} : \frac{6.57}{1} : \frac{58.39}{80} = 2.92{:}6.57{:}0.734$$

$$= 4{:}9{:}1$$

Empirical formula of *B* is C_4H_9Br.

(b) Structures of:

A

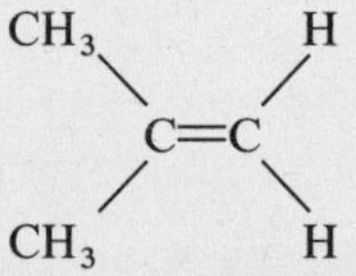

B

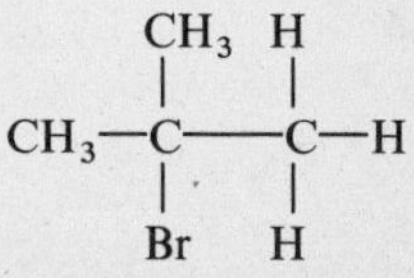

C 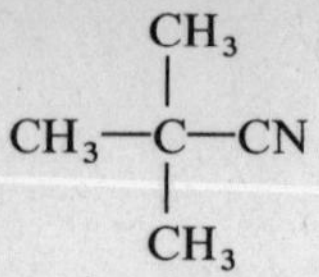 *D* 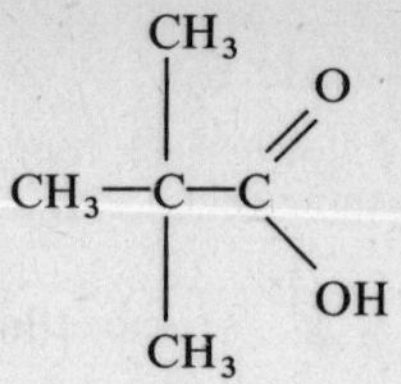

(c) Heat the nitrile under reflux with excess dil aqueous acid (alternatively, heat under reflux with excess aqueous alkali, cool and acidify the product).

(d) 1 mol C_4H_8 should give 1 mol $C_5H_{10}O_2$.

$5.6\,\ell\ C_4H_8$, at stp$=\frac{5.6}{22.4}=\frac{1}{4}$ mol

$Mr(C_5H_{10}O_2)=(5\times 12)+10+(2\times 16)=102$

$\frac{1}{4}$ mol $C_5H_{10}O$ should give $\frac{1}{4}\times 102$ g $C_5H_{10}O_2$.

$=25.5$ g $C_5H_{10}O_2$

% yield of $D=\frac{8.5}{25.5}\times 100\%=33.3\%$

(e) 2-methylbutanoic acid might be obtained either from $CH_3.CH_2.CH{=}CH_2$ (but-1-ene) or from $CH_3.CH{=}CH.CH_3$ (but-2-ene).

Example 6

Describe how you would carry out any FOUR of the following conversions. Balanced equations are not required, but you should give reagents, structures of intermediate compounds and, as far as possible, conditions of reactions. You should try to accomplish each conversion in no more than four stages.

(a) $CH_2{=}CH_2$ to CH_2COOH | CH_2COOH

(b) $CH_3.CHBr.CH_3$ to $CH_3.CHBr.CH_2Br$

(c) C_6H_6 to $C_6H_5.COOH$

(d) $C_2H_5.CN$ to C_2H_5OH

(e) $C_2H_5.COOH$ to $C_2H_5NH_2$

(f) C_6H_6 to $C_6H_5.NH.CO.CH_3$ (L)

Answer

(a)

$$\begin{array}{c}CH_2\\ \| \\ CH_2\end{array} \xrightarrow{Br_2} \begin{array}{c}CH_2Br\\ | \\ CH_2Br\end{array} \xrightarrow{KCN} \begin{array}{c}CH_2.CN\\ | \\ CH_2.CN\end{array} \xrightarrow{aq\,H^+} \begin{array}{c}CH_2.COOH\\ | \\ CH_2.COOH\end{array}$$

This synthesis may be carried out first by passing the ethene into bromine covered by a thin layer of water. The dibromo compound formed is then refluxed with potassium cyanide in ethanol, the resultant product being hydrolysed, by refluxing with excess dil aqueous acid giving the butanedioic acid.

(b)

$$CH_3.CHBr.CH_3 \xrightarrow{KOH} CH_3.CH{=}CH_2 \xrightarrow{Br_2} CH_3.CHBr.CH_2Br$$

The 2-bromopropane should be heated with potassium hydroxide in ethanol and the gaseous product passed into liquid bromine covered by a thin layer of water, the product being 1,2-dibromopropane.

(c)

$$C_6H_6 \xrightarrow{CH_3I} C_6H_5.CH_3 \xrightarrow{MnO_4^-/OH^-} C_6H_5.COOH$$

Benzene is converted to methyl benzene by refluxing with iodomethane using aluminium chloride (anhydrous) as catalyst (Friedel–Crafts reaction). The methylbenzene is then oxidized to benzoic acid by refluxing with an excess of alkaline potassium manganate(VII), which is reduced to manganate(VI).

(d)

$$C_2H_5.CN \xrightarrow{H_2O} C_2H_5.C\begin{array}{l} {/\!\!/}O \\ \diagdown NH_2\end{array} \xrightarrow{Br_2/OH^-}$$

$$C_2H_5.NH_2 \xrightarrow{H^+(aq)\,NO_2^-} C_2H_5OH$$

Careful hydrolysis of the nitrile, using mildly alkaline conditions gives propanamide. Bromine is added to this, the dil sodium hydroxide added in excess. On warming, ethylamine is evolved. This is absorbed in excess dil hydrochloric acid. Sodium nitrite solution is added to this, reacting to give ethanol.

(e)

$$C_2H_5.COOH \xrightarrow{PCl_5} C_2H_5.COCl \xrightarrow{NH_3}$$

$$C_2H_5.CONH_2 \xrightarrow{Br_2/OH^-} C_2H_5NH_2.$$

Reaction of the acid with phosphorus(V) chloride at room temperature gives propanoyl chloride. This, when reacted at room temperature with conc aqueous ammonia gives the amide. Addition of bromine to this followed by excess dil alkali, followed by warming results in the evolution of ethylamine.

(f)

$$C_6H_6 \xrightarrow{HNO_3/H_2SO_4} C_6H_5.NO_2 \xrightarrow{Sn/HCl}$$

$$C_6H_5.NH_2 \xrightarrow{(CH_3.CO)_2O} C_6H_5.NH.CO.CH_3$$

Benzene is nitrated by reaction with a mixture of conc nitric and conc sulphuric acids (1:1), the temperature being kept below 50°C to prevent formation of the dinitro compound. The product is reduced using tin and conc hydrochloric acid—this is added at room temperature, the mixture being shaken during addition in reflux apparatus, and being warmed, if necessary, to initiate reaction of the metal and the acid. The phenylamine produced is finally reacted with a 1:1 mixture of ethanoic anhydride and ethanoic acid in reflux apparatus. The mixture is refluxed gently for a while, cooled and then poured into water. The solid product that separates is *N*-phenylethanamide.

Example 7

(a) Poly(ethene) (Polythene) is a *polymer*.

(i) Explain the term *polymer*. 1 *mark*

(ii) Write the structural formula of poly(ethene). 2 *marks*

(iii) State the conditions under which poly(ethene) may be formed. 2 *marks*

(iv) To which class of polymers does poly(ethene) belong? Give reasons for your answer. 2 *marks*

(v) Give a large scale use of poly(ethene) and state one property of the polymer which makes it suitable for that use. 2 *marks*

(b) Benzene-1,4-dicarboxylic acid (terephthalic acid) and ethane-1,2-diol (ethylene glycol) polymerize under appropriate conditions.

(i) To which class of polymers does the product belong? Give an explanation. 2 *marks*

(ii) Write the structural formulae of each of the two monomers and of the polymer. 4 *marks*

(AEB: Nov 1978)

Answer

(a) **(i)** A polymer is a substance having the same molecular formula as the monomer (building unit), but its molecular formula is a multiple of that of the monomer.

(ii)

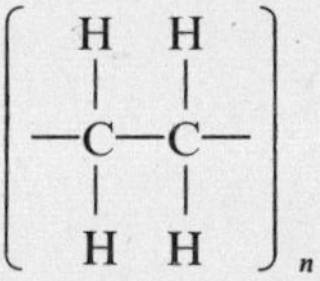

(iii) By heating under pressure with a trace of oxygen (or heating with a complex organic catalyst at ordinary pressure).

(iv) Poly(ethene) is an addition polymer, as no substance is eliminated in the polymerization.

(v) It is used for packaging (bottles, film, etc.) as it is both inert and flexible.

(b) **(i)** The product is a condensation polymer as water is eliminated during the formation of the polyester.

(ii)

$HOCH_2.CH_2OH$

Benzene-1,4-dicarboxylic acid   Ethane-1,2-diol

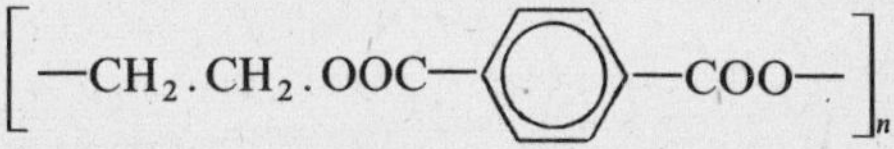

Terylene (a polyester)

Example 8

The following table lists the relative molecular masses and boiling points of some organic compounds:

Compound	Relative molecular mass	Boiling point/K
Benzene	78	353
Methylbenzene	92	383
Phenol	94	454
Nitrobenzene	123	483
2-Nitrophenol	139	494
4-Nitrophenol	139	518

(a) What reason(s) can you suggest for the *general* rise in boiling point with increasing relative molecular mass of these compounds? *2 marks*

(b) Why does water not fit into the pattern of the table? *1 mark*

(c) (i) Draw the structural formulae of 2-nitrophenol and 4-nitrophenol.

(ii) Suggest a reason why the boiling point of 4-nitrophenol is higher than that of 2-nitrophenol.

(iii) Which of the two isomers is likely to be more soluble in water? Give reason. *7 marks*

(NUFF)

Answer

(a) With increasing molecular mass there is also an increase in the number of electrons in the molecule. The strength of Van der Waals forces increases with increasing number of electrons. It is these forces which have to be overcome on boiling, hence the increased b.p. with increasing relative molecular mass.

(b) Water is a highly polar molecule in which hydrogen is bonded to the small electronegative oxygen. This results in a greater attraction between molecules (hydrogen bonding).

(c) (i) 2-Nitrophenol 4-Nitrophenol

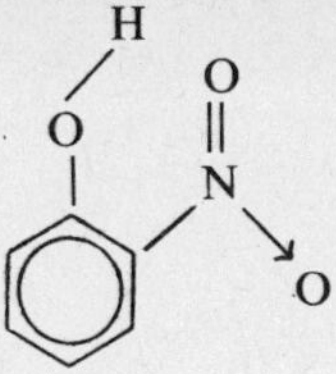

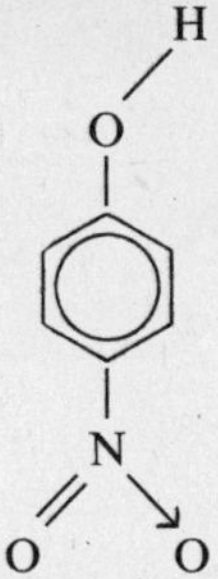

(ii) Intramolecular hydrogen bonding occurs in the 2-isomer, whereas the only attraction in the 4-isomer is between one molecule and another.

(iii) The 4-isomer is likely to be the more soluble as both functional groups are available to hydrogen bond with water. The intramolecular hydrogen bonding in the 2-isomer restricts the amount of hydrogen bonding which can occur with water.

Example 9

For each of the following pairs of isomeric compounds, suggest an experimental procedure, based on chemical tests, which could be used to distinguish between the members of each pair. The expected observations should be clearly described, and equations given where appropriate.

(a) $CH_3.CO.CH_3$ and $CH_3.CH_2.CHO$

(b) $CH_3.CH_2.CH_2OH$ and $CH_3.CHOH.CH_3$

(c) $(CH_3)_3.CBr$ and $CH_3.CH_2.CH_2.CH_2Br$

(d) $CH_3.CH_2.CH_2.CH_2OH$ and $C_2H_5.O.C_2H_5$

(e) CH_3—  —NH_2 and  —CH_2NH_2

(L)

Answer

(a) $CH_3.CO.CH_3$ and $CH_3.CH_2.CHO$

These may be distinguished because propanone has no reducing properties but propanol, which can easily be oxidized to propanoic acid, will reduce a number of oxidizing agents. Addition of acidified dichromate(VI) and warming the mixture will give no colour change with propanone, but will change from orange to green when reacted with propanal:

$$CH_3.CH_2.CHO + [O] \rightarrow CH_3.CH_2.COOH$$

Alternative oxidizing agents include (i) copper(II) complex in alkaline solution (Fehling's or Benedict's solutions) reduced to copper(I) oxide; (ii) silver(I) complex with ammonia, reduced to silver; (iii) acidified manganate(VII); alternative tests include (iv) aqueous sodium hydroxide—no reaction with the ketone; formation of a yellow resin on heating with the aldehyde; (v) heating with sodium hydroxide and iodine [or sodium chlorate(I) and potassium iodide] which gives yellow crystalline triiodomethane with the ketone, as it contains a $CH_3.C{-}O$ group, but no reaction with the aldehyde. This last test is not recommended, as it is best used for (b) below.

(b) $CH_3.CH_2.CH_2OH$ and $CH_3.CHOH.CH_3$

Propan-1-ol does not contain a $CH_3{-}C{-}O$ group whereas propan-2-ol does. These two may therefore be distinguished by adding sodium hydroxide solution to iodine solution until the colour just disappears. The organic compound is then added and the mixture warmed in a water bath. On cooling, yellow crystals of triiodomethane would be observed with propan-2-ol, whereas propan-1-ol would not react:

$$CH_3.CHOH.CH_3 + [O] \rightarrow CH_3.CO.CH_3 + H_2O$$

$$CH_3.CO.CH_3 + 3I_2 \rightarrow CI_3.CO.CH_3$$

$$CI_3.CO.CH_3 + H_2O \rightarrow CHI_3 + CH_3.COOH$$

(c) $(CH_3)_3.CBr$ and $CH_3.CH_2.CH_2.CH_2Br$

2-Bromo-2-methylpropane is a tertiary halide, whereas 1-bromobutane is a primary halide. These therefore hydrolyse at different rates. Addition of aqueous silver nitrate, followed by warming may therefore be used as a test to distinguish between them. The tertiary halide hydrolyses much more readily than the primary compound, so a pale cream ppte of silver bromide will be observed first with this substance. 1-Bromobutane would only give a ppte on much more prolonged warming:

$$(CH_3)_3.CBr + H_2O \rightarrow (CH_3)_3.COH + HBr \text{ (fast)}$$

$$HBr(aq) + Ag^+(aq) \rightarrow AgBr(s) + H^+(aq)$$

$$CH_3.CH_2.CH_2.CH_2Br + H_2O \rightarrow CH_3.CH_2.CH_2.CH_2OH + HBr \text{ (slow)}$$

An alternative method would be to hydrolyse each by refluxing with aqueous alkali and then adding excess acid and potassium dichromate(VI). On warming, there would be no reaction with the product of hydrolysis of the tertiary halide as tertiary alcohols do not oxidize, whereas the primary alcohol obtained by hydrolysis of the primary halide would reduce the orange dichromate(VI) to green chromium(III).

(d) $CH_3.CH_2.CH_2.CH_2OH$ and $C_2H_5.O.C_2H_5$

Addition of a small piece of sodium metal would be a suitable reaction. The alcohol reacts, producing hydrogen, with effervescence:

$$2CH_3.CH_2.CH_2.CH_2OH + 2Na \rightarrow 2CH_3.CH_2.CH_2.CH_2ONa + H_2$$

The ether does not react.

Alternative reactions are (i) the addition of phosphorus(V) chloride—the alcohol gives hydrogen chloride (white fumes in moist air), whereas the dry ether does not react; or (ii) adding ethanoic acid and a few drops conc sulphuric acid and warming—the alcohol gives a sweet smelling ester—the ether does not react; or (iii) adding acidified dichromate(VI)—the alcohol reduces the dichromate (from orange to green)—the ether does not react.

(e)

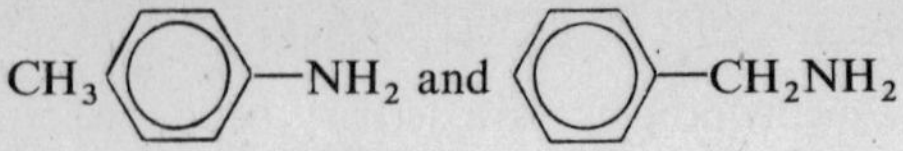

Each substance is dissolved in excess dil sulphuric acid and the resultant solution cooled to less than 5°C. A solution of sodium nitrite, also cooled to below 5°C, is then added slowly, maintaining the low temperature. 4-methylphenylamine gives a yellow diazonium salt, which, on addition of phenol dissolved in sodium hydroxide gives an orange azo dye:

(i)

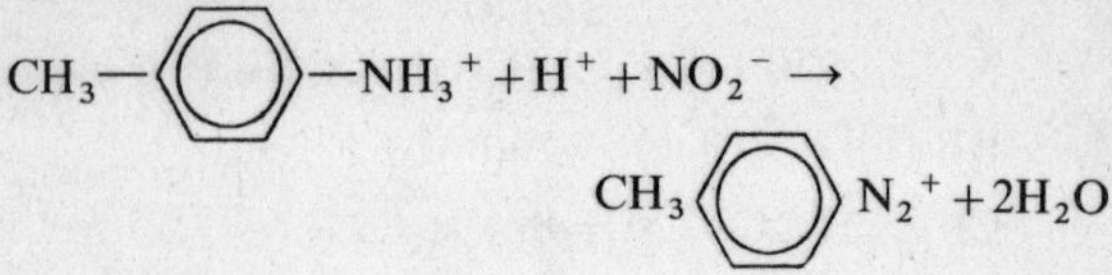

(ii)

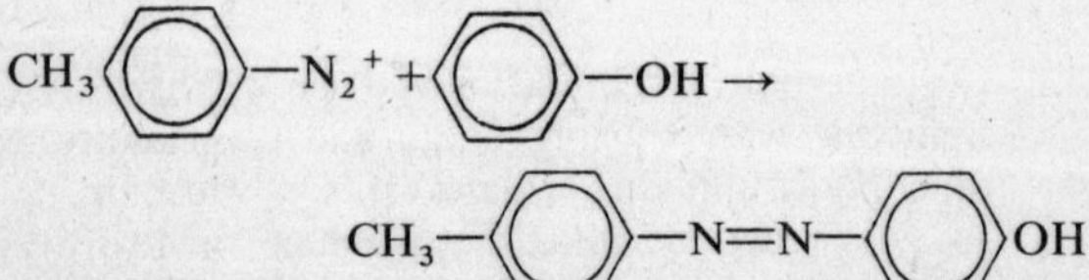

Aminomethylbenzene reacts with the nitrite, even at low temperature, to produce nitrogen gas, and leaves a colourless product, as the amino group is attached to an alkyl carbon atom:

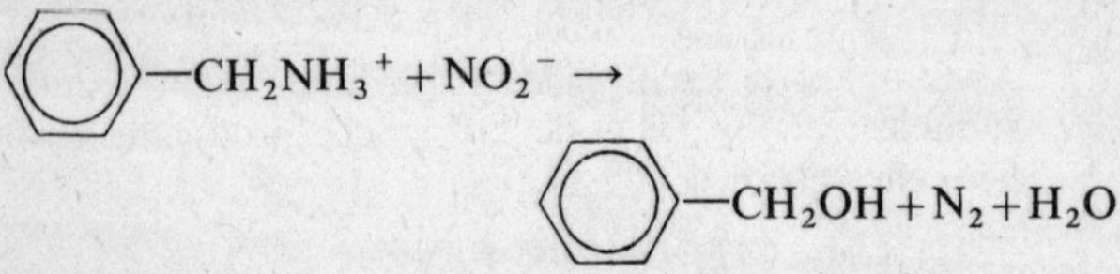

An alternative reaction is addition of bromine water: the aromatic amine gives a white ppte of the bromo derivative, rapidly decolorizing the bromine water—the alkylamine does not react.

Example 10

A compound *P* contains carbon 59.4%, hydrogen 10.9%, nitrogen 13.9% and oxygen 15.8%, by mass. (Relative atomic masses: H = 1, C = 12, N = 14, O = 16.)

On distilling P with hot dil aqueous sodium hydroxide Q, C_2H_7N is formed immediately and R, $C_3H_6O_2$, when the residual solution is acidified. A colourless gas and a liquid S are formed on treating Q with an ice-cold solution of sodium nitrite and dil sulphuric acid. On warming with S and a few drops of concentrated sulphuric acid, R forms a sweet smelling liquid T.

Identify P, Q, R, S and T and write equations for the reactions described.

How would you prepare P, using Q and R as starting materials?

Give the structure of any FOUR isomers of P containing the same function group as P.

(L)

Answer

Compound P: ratio $C:H:N:O = \frac{59.4}{12}:\frac{10.9}{1}:\frac{13.9}{14}:\frac{15.8}{16}$

$= 4.95:10.9:0.993:0.988$

$\div$ by 0.988 $= 5:10:1:1$
(to nearest whole No.)

Empirical formula of P is $C_5H_{10}NO$.

As P gives, on hydrolysis, a 2-carbon and a 3-carbon product, the former nitrogen containing, the latter a carboxylic acid (initially as its salt) it has the structure

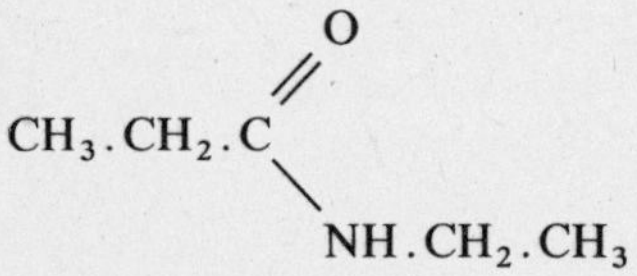

N-Ethylpropanamide

Q contains an amino group $—NH_2$ as it produces a colourless gas, nitrogen, on reaction with sodium nitrite and dilute acid.

Q is: $CH_3.CH_2.NH_2$ Ethylamine

R is a carboxylic acid, reacting with *S* (an alcohol) to give an ester (a sweet smelling liquid). It has the structure:

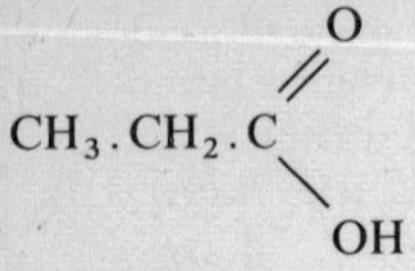

Propanoic acid

S is an alcohol, as the reaction of an amine with a nitrite and acid replaces the $-NH_2$ group by $-OH$.

S is: $CH_3.CH_2OH$ Ethanol

T is the ester formed by reaction of *S* with *R*, ie, it is:

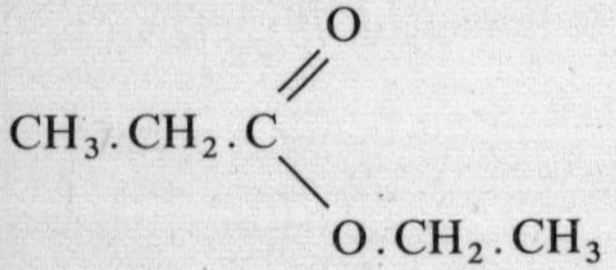

Ethylpropionate

Equations for the reactions are:

(i) $\underset{(P)}{CH_3.CH_2.CONH.CH_2.CH_3} + OH^- \rightarrow \underset{\text{(salt of } R)}{CH_3.CH_2.COO^-} + \underset{(Q)}{CH_3.CH_2.NH_2}$

(ii) $\underset{(Q)}{CH_3.CH_2NH_2} + H^+ + NO_2^- \rightarrow \underset{(S)}{CH_3.CH_2OH} + N_2 + H_2O$

(iii) $\underset{(R)}{CH_3.CH_2.COOH} + \underset{(S)}{CH_3.CH_2OH} \overset{H^+}{\rightleftharpoons} \underset{(T)}{CH_3.CH_2.COO.CH_2.CH_3} + H_2O$

Preparation of P from Q and R

(i) The first step is the preparation of propanoyl chloride by reaction of the acid with phosphorus(V) chloride (or sulphur dichloride oxide).

$$CH_3.CH_2.COOH + PCl_5 \rightarrow CH_3.CH_2.COCl + POCl_3 + HCl$$

(ii) This is then added a little at a time to the ethylamine, forming the product *P*:

$$CH_3.CH_2.COCl + CH_3.CH_2NH_2 \rightarrow CH_3.CH_2.CO.NH.CH_2.CH_3 + HCl$$

Four isomers of P containing the amide link

(i)

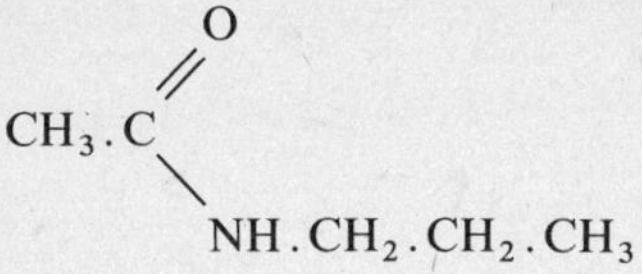

(ii)

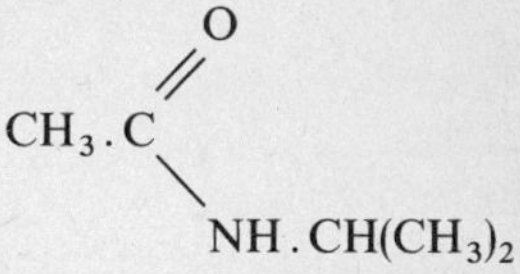

(iii)

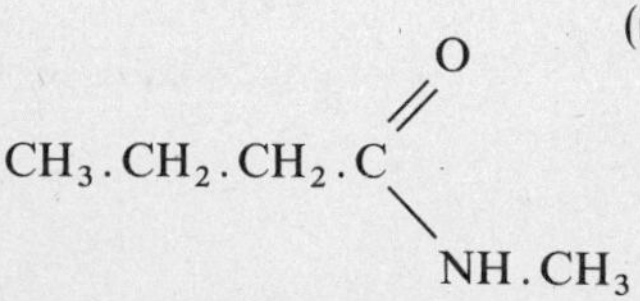

(iv)

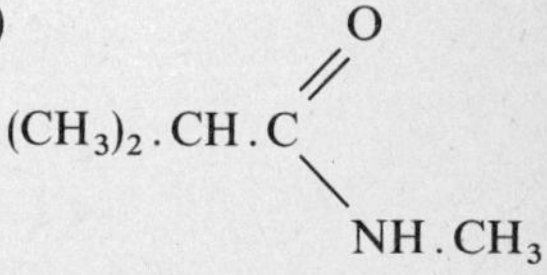

Example 11

(a) Write a systematic name for each of the following compounds:

A $CH_3.CH(OH).CH_2.CH_3$

B $(CH_3)_3.CBr$

C $CH_3.CH_2.CH_2.CHO$

D $CH_3.CH_2.CH{=}CH_2$

E $HOOC.CH_2.CH_2.COOH$ 5 *marks*

(b) Use the letters *A* to *E* to refer to the compounds (if any) that:

(i) exhibit optical isomerism.

(ii) react with conc sulphuric acid to form an alkene.

(iii) polymerize under appropriate conditions.

3 *marks*

(c) Which two compounds, *A* to *E*, react to form:

(i) an ester.

(ii) an acetal? *4 marks*

(d) Give the mechanism for the reaction of:

(i) *D* with bromine.

(ii) *B* with aqueous alkali. *6 marks*

(L)

Answer

(a) *A* is butan-2-ol.

B is 2-bromo-2-methylpropane.

C is butanal.

D is but-1-ene.

E is butanedioic acid.

(b) **(i)** *A* only (it contains an asymmetrically substituted carbon atom).

(ii) *A* only (alcohols dehydrate to alkenes).

(iii) *D* only (contains a double bond).

(c) **(i)** *A* and *E* react to form an ester (alcohol and acid react to give an ester).

(ii) *C* and *A* (acetals are formed by reaction of an aldehyde and an alcohol).

(d) **(i)**

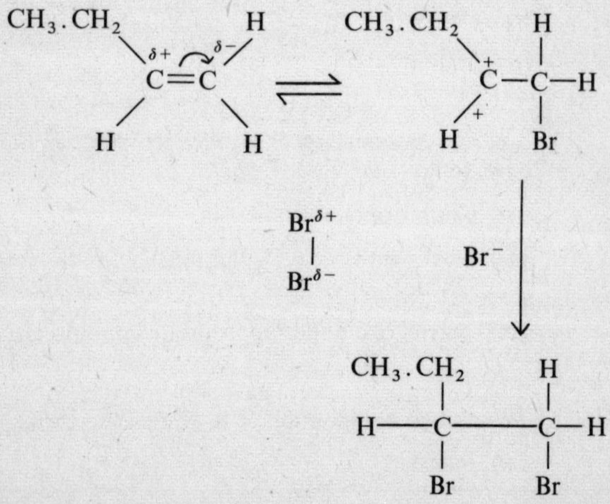

(ii)

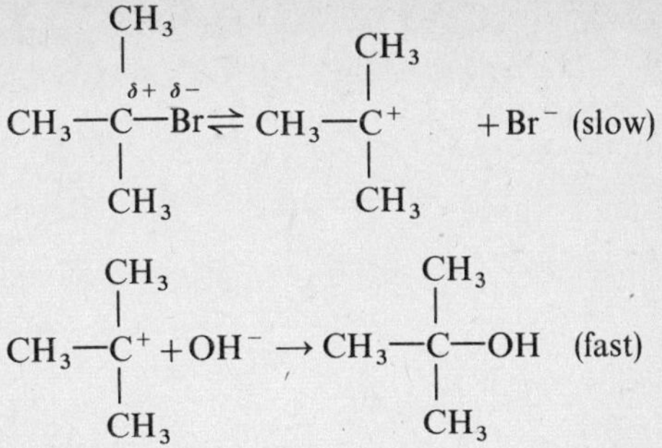

Example 12

This question is about three hydrocarbons whose formulae are:

A

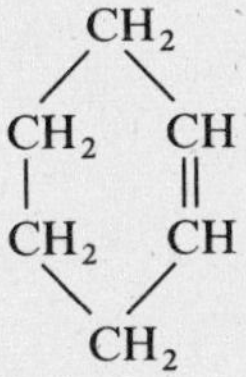

B

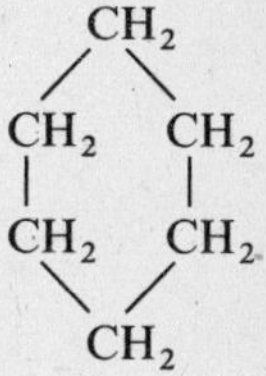

C

(a) Give the names of the hydrocarbons *B* and *C*.

2 *marks*

(b) Each of the compounds will react with bromine in the ratio 1 mol compound: 1 mol Br. Complete the following table:

Compound	Conditions for reacting with Br	Formula of organic product	Type of attack on organic compound (nucleophilic/ electrophilic/ free radical)
A			
B			
C			

9 *marks*

(c) Describe, giving reagents and reaction conditions, how *B* may be converted into:

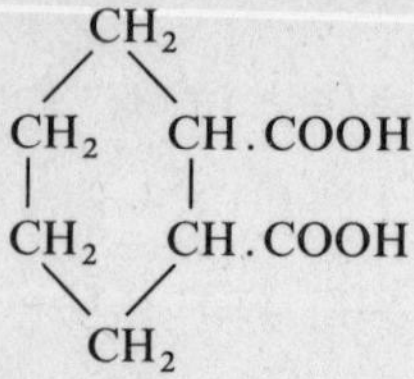

5 *marks*

(d) The enthalpies of formation, ΔH_c, of *B* and *C* are -52 and $-156\,kJ\,mol^{-1}$, respectively. Calculate the enthalpy of hydrogenation of *B*, giving your reasoning.

3 *marks*

(L)

Answer

(a) *B* is cyclohexene

C is cyclohexane.

(b)

Compound	Conditions for reacting	Formula of organic product	Type of attack on organic compound (nucleophilic/ electrophilic/ free radical)
A	Iron or $AlCl_3$ catalyst. Room temp & pressure		Electrophilic substitution
B	Br_2 in $CHCl_3$	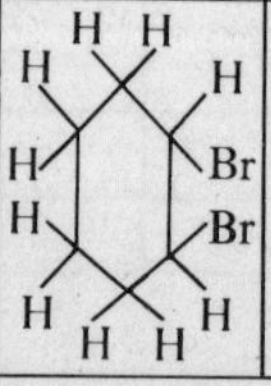	Electrophilic addition

C	Pure bromine uv radiation	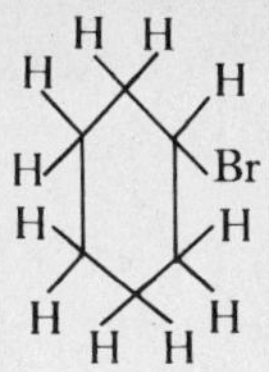	Free radical substitution

(c) React *B* with bromine in $CHCl_3$. To the adduct add conc aqueous potassium cyanide to replace the halogen by the nitrile group.

This is then hydrolysed by refluxing with excess dil hydrochloric acid, giving the required product.

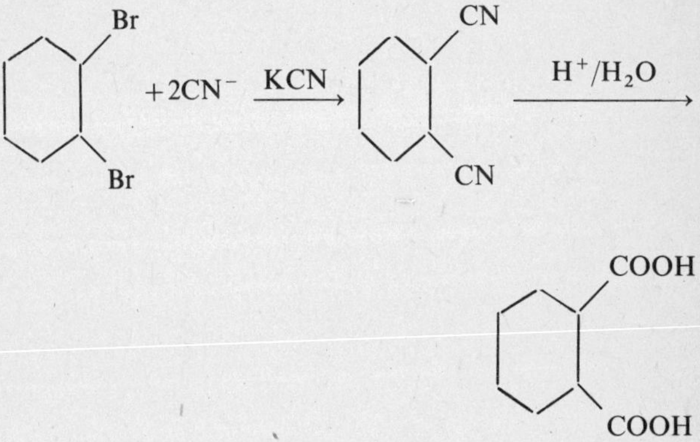

(d)

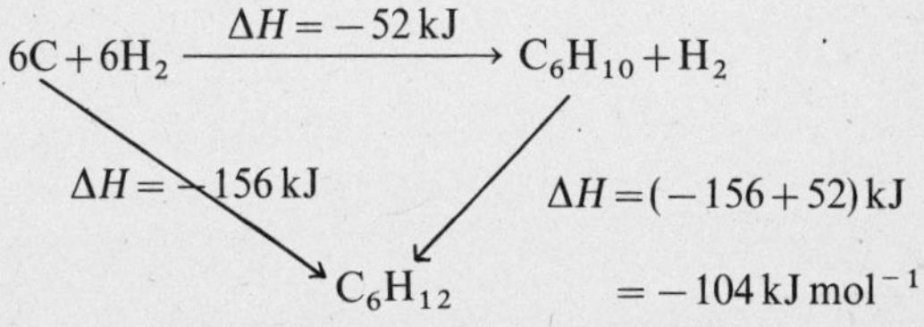

Example 13

This question concerns the following isomeric alkenes:

A 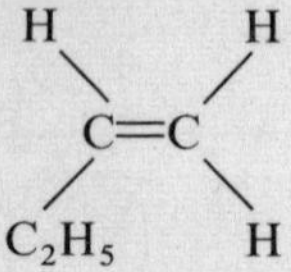

B 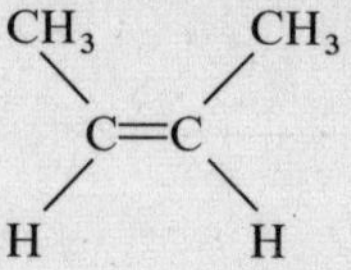

C 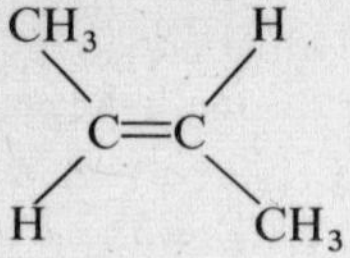

D 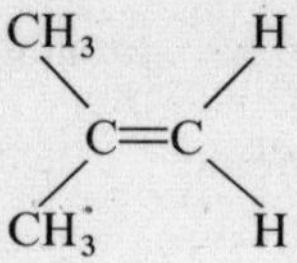

(a) Give the names of *A*, *B*, *C* and *D*.

2 *marks*

(b) (i) What kind of isomerism is shown by *B* and *C*?

(ii) How do you account for the separate existence of *B* and *C*?

(iii) Give the structure(s) of the compound(s) that would be formed when *B* and *C* react separately with bromine.

How would you carry out this reaction in the laboratory?

5 *marks*

(c) The reaction of hydrogen bromide with *A* gives 2-bromobutane as the major product.

(i) What conditions would you use to carry out this reaction?

(i) Give a mechanism for the reaction.

(iii) Give the structure of the major product you would expect from the reaction of *D* with hydrogen bromide.

6 *marks*

(L)

Answer

(a) *A* is but-1-ene.
B is *cis*-but-2-ene.
C is *trans*-but-2-ene.
D is methylpropene.

(b) **(i)** *B* and *C* are geometric isomers.

(ii) They exist as the double bond restricts free rotation so that the methyl groups are fixed relative to each other.

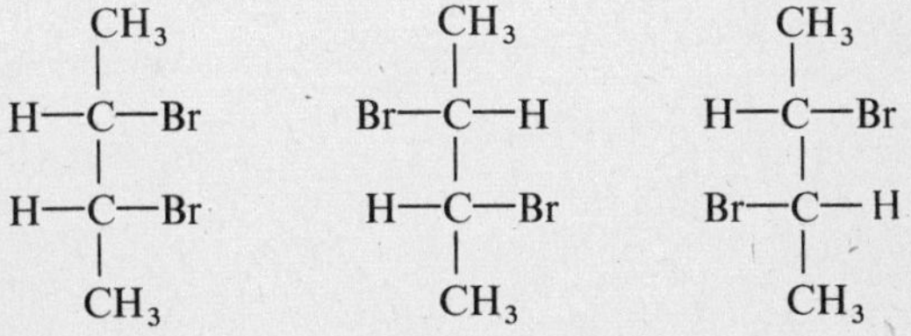

Both *B* and *C* would give mixtures containing the above stereo isomers.

The reaction would be carried out by bubbling the gases through bromine dissolved in a non-polar solvent, eg, trichloromethane.

(c) **(i)** The gas could be bubbled through conc aqueous hydrogen bromide (or mixed with anhydrous hydrogen bromide gas).

(ii)

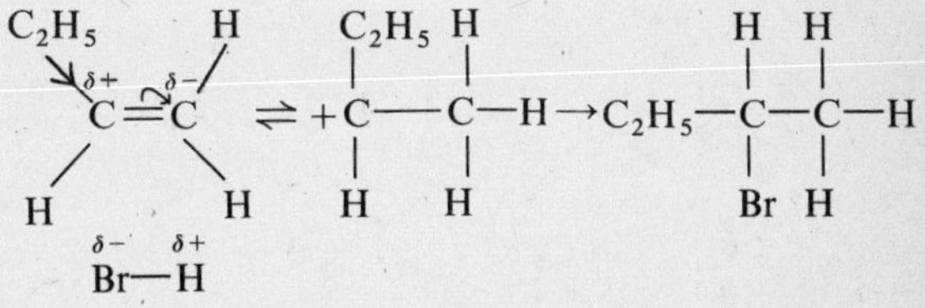

(iii) *D* would give

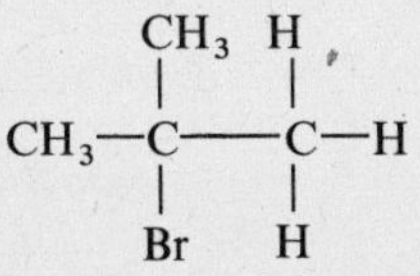

Example 14

(a) For each of parts (i) to (viii) below ONE OR MORE of the alternatives *A*, *B*, *C* and *D* listed below are correct. Decide which of the alternatives is (are) correct and write the appropriate letters in answer to the question.

A $CH_3.CHO$ *B* $C_6H_5.CHO$

C HCHO *D* $C_6H_5.CO.CH_3$

(i) Which could be prepared by oxidation of a primary alcohol?

(ii) Which will polymerize on evaporation of an aqueous solution?

(iii) Which will give a yellow precipitate on warming with a mixture of iodine and alkali?

(iv) Which will disproportionate on treatment with strong aqueous alkali?

(v) Which will reduce complexed Cu^{2+} ions in alkaline solution to a precipitate of Cu_2O?

(vi) Which will give a mixture of optical isomers on treatment with potassium cyanide solution followed by dil hydrochloric acid?

(vii) Which could be reduced to an alcohol by hydrogen in the presence of a nickel catalyst?

(viii) Which could undergo an addition reaction with chlorine? 20 *marks*

(b) What do you understand by the term *condensation reaction*? Illustrate your answer with an equation. 4 *marks*

(c) The reaction of anhydrous hydrogen cyanide with propanone is slow, but on addition of a little aqueous alkali the reaction proceeds rapidly. What explanation can you offer for these observations? 6 *marks*

(SUJB)

Answer

(a) **(i)** *A*, *B* and *C* (aldehydes are obtained by oxidation of primary alcohols).

(ii) *C* (methanal polymerizes on evaporation).

(iii) *A* and *D* (these contain a $CH_3.C{-}O$ group, and react to give triiodomethane).

(iv) *B* and *C* both disproportionate (they do not have an α C—H bond).

(v) *A*, *B* and *C* all reduce complexed Cu^{2+} ions (they are aldehydes, with reducing properties).

(vi) *A*, *B* and *D* all give a mixture of optical isomers (the adducts, on hydrolysis all are (2-)hydroxy carboxylic acids, with four different groups on the (2-)carbon atom).

(vii) *A*, *B*, *C* and *D* can all be reduced to alcohols.

(viii) *B* and *D* (of the compounds listed, only those with an aromatic nucleus are capable of forming an addition product).

(b) A condensation reaction is one in which two or more substances react to give a product by the elimination of water, or other simple substance. An example is the reaction of a carbonyl compound with hydroxylamine to form an oxime:

$$CH_3.CH{=}O + H_2NOH \rightarrow CH_2.CH{=}NOH + H_2O$$

Ethanal — Ethanal oxime

(c) The reaction involves initial nucleophilic attack of the carbon atom of the carbonyl group. Hydrogen cyanide, a weak acid, does not polarize readily, so that the initial attack is slow. The addition of a little alkali results in formation of the cyanide ion which is the nucleophile in this reaction.

(i)

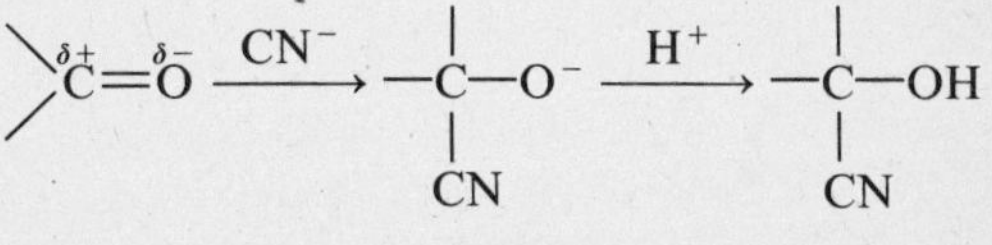

(ii) $HCN + OH^- \rightarrow H_2O + CN^-$

Example 15

(a) Explain in terms of molecular structure each of the following types of isomerism. In each case give one example (two isomers) and outline one method, either chemical or physical, by which the isomers in your example might be distinguished:

(i) Structural isomerism.

(ii) Geometric isomerism.

(iii) Optical isomerism. *12 marks*

(b) (i) The compound 2-iodobutane is a *secondary* alkyl iodide. Explain what is meant by secondary.

(ii) Which of the compounds, $CH_3.(CH_2)_3I$, $C_2H_5.(CH_3)CHI$ and $(CH_3)_3.CI$ will be hydrolysed by OH^- ions most quickly, and which most slowly? *3 marks*

(c) State how you would bring about the following transformations, giving reagents and conditions:

(i) $CH_3.(CH_2)_3I$ to $CH_3.(CH_2)_3.COOH$.

(ii) $CH_3.(CH_2)_3.COOH$ to $CH_3.(CH_2)_3I$. *7 marks*

(L)

Answer

(a) **(i)** Structural isomerism results from atoms being arranged differently in a molecule. Substances have the same molecular formula but different structural formulae. Example:

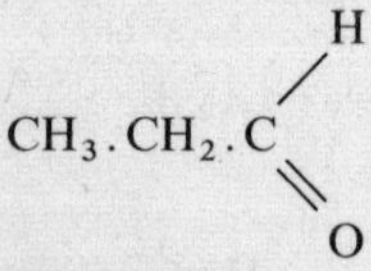

$CH_3.CO.CH_3$

Propanal Propanone

Distinction: The (+) isomer, when in aqueous solution, dichromate(VI) on warming, changing its colour from orange to green; propanone does not react as it cannot be oxidized.

(ii) Geometric isomerism occurs when free rotation about a carbon—carbon bond is restricted and two dissimilar groups are attached to the carbon atoms of that bond. The restriction to free rotation can be caused by a double bond. Example:

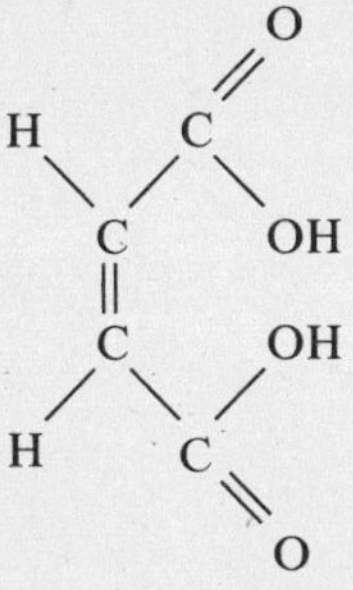

cis-But-2-enedioic acid

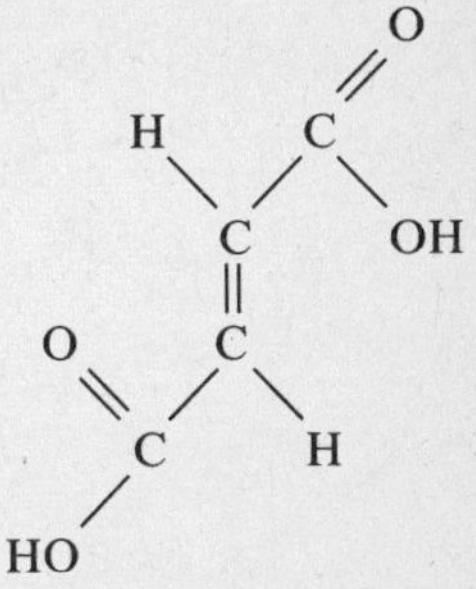

trans-But-2-enedioic acid

Distinction: The *cis*-isomer forms an anhydride by loss of water at just over 100°C; the *trans*-isomer only forms the identical anhydride by heating more strongly.

(iii) Optical isomerism occurs when four different groups are attached to one carbon atom. These can adopt different relative positions in space, one structure being a non-superimposable mirror image of the other. Example:

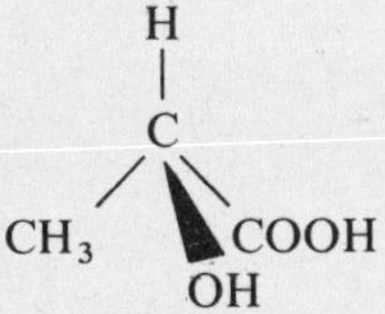

(+) 2-Hydroxypropanoic acid

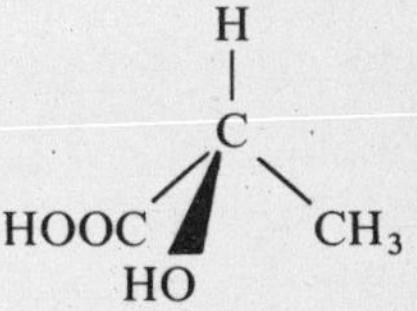

(−) 2-hydroxypropanoic acid

Distinction: The (+) isomer, when in aqueous solution, will rotate the plane of monochromatic plane polarized light to the right; the (−) isomer will rotate the light the same angle but to the left.

(b) (i) The carbon atom to which the iodine is attached has two alkyl groups also attached to it.

(ii) Fastest: $(CH_3)_3.Cl$ Slowest: $CH_3.(CH_2)_3I$

(c) (i) This is brought about by firstly reacting it with potassium cyanide in ethanol to give the nitrile, which is then hydrolysed by refluxing with excess aqueous acid (eg, HCl).

$$CH_3.(CH_2)_3I \xrightarrow[\text{(in ethanol)}]{\text{KCN}} CH_3.(CH_2)_3.CN$$

$$\xrightarrow[\text{reflux}]{H^+\text{(aq)}} CH_3.(CH_2)_3.COOH$$

(ii) This is done by reaction of the acid with solid phosphorus(V) chloride and reaction of the product with conc aqueous ammonia to give the amide. This then has bromine followed by potassium hydroxide dissolved in ethanol added. On warming, an amine is evolved which is absorbed in excess dil acid. The salt is then reacted with aqueous sodium nitrite, giving an alcohol. This is finally reacted with moist red phosphorus and iodine to give the iodo compound:

$$CH_3.(CH_2)_3.COOH \xrightarrow{PCl_5}$$

$$CH_3.(CH_2)_3.COCl \xrightarrow{NH_3} CH_3.(CH_2)_3.CONH_2$$

$$\downarrow Br_2/OH^-$$

$$CH_3.(CH_2)_3I \xleftarrow{\text{red } P/I_2}$$

$$CH_3.(CH_2)_3OH \xleftarrow{H^+/NO_2^-} CH_3.(CH_2)_3NH_2$$

Example 16

The substance *methyl orange* can be made by diazotizing 'sulphanilic acid' (4-aminobenzenesulphonic acid) and coupling the product with 'dimethylaniline' (*N,N*-dimethylphenylamine). The structure of the latter is:

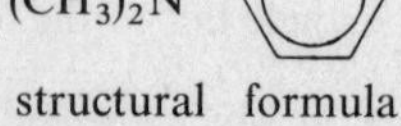

(a) Give the structural formula of 4-aminobenzene-sulphonic acid. 1 *mark*

(b) The diazotization is carried out by dissolving the 4-aminobenzenesulphonic acid in sodium carbonate solution, adding sodium nitrite solution and cooling to below 7°C. Some concentrated hydrochloric acid is also cooled, and then added slowly to the solution.

(i) It is important that the temperature should be maintained between 5° and 10°C while the acid is being added. Explain why this is so.

(ii) Why does the diazotization not start until the acid is added?

(iii) Write an equation for the diazotization, and give the structural formula of the diazonium compound. 5 *marks*

(c) While the mixture from (b) is allowed to stand for a few minutes, some *N*,*N*-dimethylphenylamine is dissolved in hydrochloric acid. This latter solution is then added to the mixture, and finally sodium hydroxide solution is added, causing methyl orange to be precipitated.

(i) Write the formula and name of the substance formed when *N*,*N*-dimethylphenylamine reacts with hydrochloric acid.

(ii) In the coupling reaction, one mole of diazonium compound reacts with one mole of *N*,*N*-dimethylphenylamine. Write an equation for this reaction.

(iii) In one experiment a student started with 2.5 g of 4-aminobenzenesulphonic acid and appropriate amounts of the other reagents. If he obtained 3.3 g of methyl orange, what was his percentage yield? (Relative molecular masses: 4-aminobenzenesulphonic acid = 173; methyl orange = 305.)

(iv) Suggest *two* reasons why the yield in (iii) was below theoretical. 7 *marks*

(d) (i) Diazonium salts are not usually isolated, but are used in solution. Why is it prudent to do this?

(ii) Of what chemical interest is methyl orange?

3 *marks*

(L)

Answer

(a) 4-Aminobenzenesulphonic acid is:

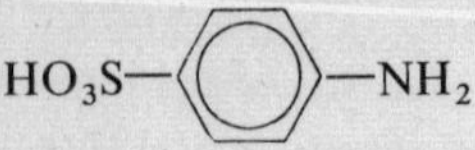

(b) (i) At too low a temperature, solubility of reagents is reduced and reaction rate is slow. At too high a temperature, the diazonium salt formed is unstable, decomposing to a phenol and nitrogen.

(ii) The reaction is of the amine group with nitrous acid, which is only formed when acid is added to a nitrite:

(iii) 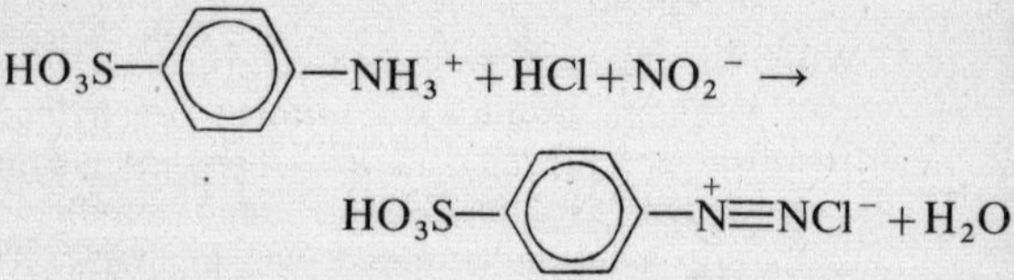

(c) (i) The product is:

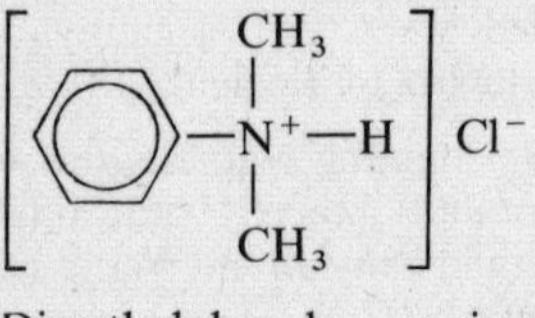

N,*N*-Dimethylphenylammonium chloride

(ii) 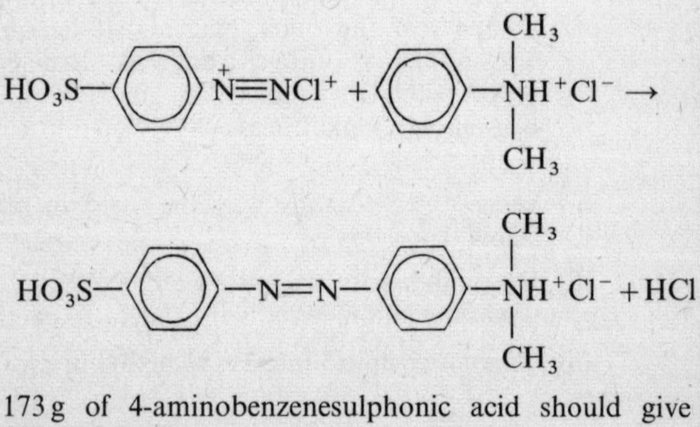

(iii) 173 g of 4-aminobenzenesulphonic acid should give 305 g of product.

$\therefore$ 2.5 g reactant should give $\frac{2.5}{173} \times 305$ g product

$$\text{Percentage yield} = \frac{\text{actual yield}}{\text{theoretical yield}} \times 100\%$$

$$= \frac{3.3 \times 173 \times 100}{2.5 \times 305} = 75\%$$

(iv) Reduced yield might be due firstly to decomposition of the diazonium salt before coupling and secondly to incomplete precipitation of the methyl orange.

(d) **(i)** These salts decompose on heating, or on drying when they may detonate.

(ii) Methyl orange may be used as an indicator.

Example 17

(a) Write the ion/electron half-equation for the reduction in acid solution of the manganate(VII) ion, MnO_4^-(aq). *2 marks*

(b) Write the ion/electron half-equation for the oxidation, in aqueous solution, of:

(i) the iron(II) ion.

(ii) the ethanedioate ion (oxalate ion), $\begin{matrix} COO^- \\ | \\ COO^- \end{matrix}$.

2 marks

(c) Write the redox equation for the reaction between manganate(VII) ions and iron(II) ethanedioate in hot acid solution.

(d) Using the equation in (c), calculate the volume of aqueous manganate(VII) ions of concentration $0.02\,mol\,\ell^{-1}$ that would just react completely, under the correct conditions, with $25.00\,cm^3$ of a solution of iron(II) ethanedioate of concentration $0.10\,mol\,\ell^{-1}$ in aqueous sulphuric acid. *4 marks*

(AEB: June 1980)

Answer

(a) $MnO_4^-(aq) + 8H^+(aq) + 5e^- \rightarrow Mn^{2+} + 4H_2O$

(b) (i) $Fe^{2+}(aq) \rightarrow Fe^{3+}(aq) + e^-$

(ii) $\begin{matrix} COO^- \\ | \\ COO^-(aq) \end{matrix} \rightarrow 2CO_2(g) + 2e^-$

(c) $3MnO_4^- + 24H^+(aq) + 5Fe(COO^-)_2(aq)$

$\rightarrow 3Mn^{2+}(aq) + 5Fe^{3+}(aq) + 10CO_2(g) + 12H_2O$

(d) From (c) $3MnO_4^- \equiv 5Fe(COO^-)_2$

$\therefore 1Fe(COO^-)_2 \equiv \frac{3}{5} MnO_4^-$

25 cm 0.10 M $Fe(COO^-)_2$ contains $\frac{25}{1000} \times 0.1$ mols,

$\therefore$ No. of mols MnO_4^- required $= \frac{3}{5} \times \frac{25}{1000} \times 0.1$

$\therefore$ Vol. of 0.02 M MnO_4^- required $= \frac{3}{5} \times \frac{25}{1000} \times 0.1 \times \frac{1000}{0.2}$

$= 75\ cm^3$

Alternatively $\frac{V_A M_A}{V_B M_B} = \frac{a}{b}$

V_A = vol MnO_4^- reqd, M_A = molar conc MnO_4^-. Similarly for V_B, M_B and b.

$$\frac{V \times 0.02}{25 \times 0.10} = \frac{3}{5}$$

$$V = \frac{3}{5} \times \frac{25 \times 0.10}{0.02} = 75\ cm^3$$

Example 18

Methyl 3-nitrobenzoate, $CH_3OOC.C_6H_4.NO_2$, can be prepared by the nitration of methyl benzoate as follows (both methyl benzoate and its nitrated derivative are non-toxic):

(I) Weigh out 2.7 g of methyl benzoate into a small flask and then dissolve it in 5 cm^3 of concentrated sulphuric acid. When the solid has dissolved, cool the mixture in ice.

Prepare the nitrating mixture by carefully adding 2 cm^3 of conc sulphuric acid to 2 cm^3 of conc nitric acid and then cool this mixture in ice also.

(II) Add the nitrating mixture dropwise to the solution of methyl benzoate. Stir the mixture and keep the temperature below 10°C.

(III) Allow the mixture to stand at room temperature for about 15 minutes and then pour the reaction mixture on to crushed ice. Stir until all the ice has melted and crystalline methyl 3-nitrobenzoate has formed.

(IV) Filter the crystals, wash them with cold water and then recrystallize them from the minimum volume of hot ethanol. Finally, dry the crystals between filter papers.

(a) Draw FULL structural formulae for methyl benzoate and methyl 3-nitrobenzoate. 4 *marks*

(b) Write an equation for the reaction that takes place during stages (II) and (III). 2 *marks*

(c) Mention TWO factors (conditions) during the preparation that help to prevent further nitration of the product. 4 *marks*

(d) Give the names and structural formulae of TWO nitrocompounds that are likely to contaminate the impure crystals of methyl 3-nitrobenzoate. 4 *marks*

(e) Why were the crystals washed with water before recrystallization? 2 *marks*

(f) Explain how the loss of product is kept to a minimum during recrystallizations. 4 *marks*

(g) Approximately how many moles of methyl benzoate

and nitric acid were used in the preparation of methyl 3-nitrobenzoate? (Assume that conc nitric acid is pure HNO_3 and that its density is $1.5\,g\,cm^{-3}$. Relative atomic masses: H = 1; C = 12; N = 14; 0 = 16.)

4 marks

(h) What is the theoretical yield of methyl 3-nitrobenzoate?

2 marks

(SUJB)

Answer

(a)

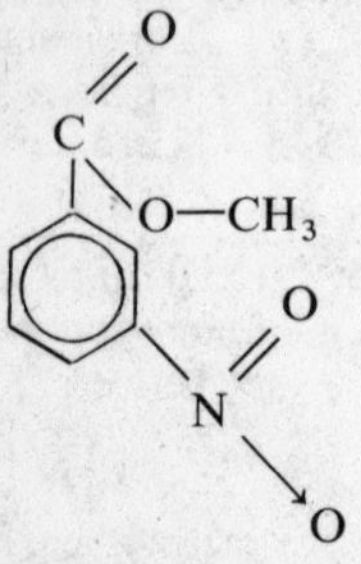

Methyl benzoate

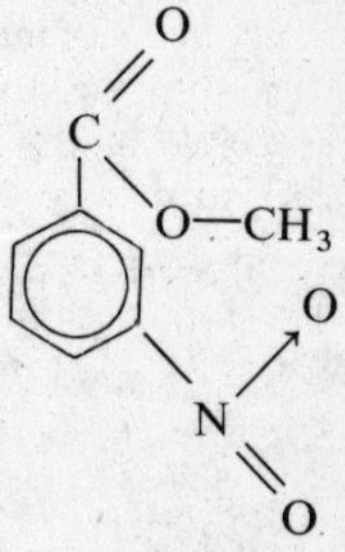

Methyl 3-nitrobenzoate

(b) $C_6H_5.COO.CH_3 + HNO_3 \xrightarrow{H_2SO_4} O_2N.C_6H_4.COO.CH_3 + H_2O$

(c) Two factors which help to prevent further nitration of the product are:

(i) keeping reagents and reaction mixture initially below 10°C during mixing.

(ii) limiting the time the reagents are allowed to react before quenching the reaction by adding to crushed ice.

(d) Two other nitro compounds likely to be formed are:

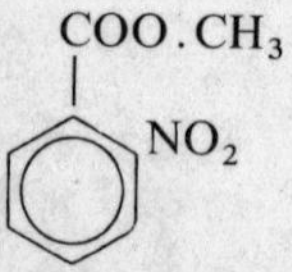

and

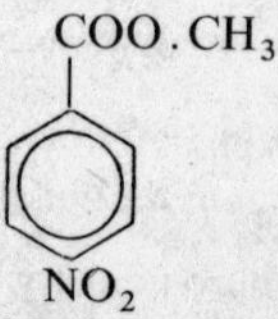

Methyl 2-nitrobenzoate

Methyl 4-nitrobenzoate

(e) The crystals were washed with water before recrystallization to remove water-soluble impurities, particularly the sulphuric acid and excess nitric acid from the nitrating mixture.

(f) Loss of product is kept to a minimum during recrystallization by

(i) careful choice of solvent—one suitable for the material being recrystallized is used.

(ii) use of minimum amount of solvent so that as much as possible of the solute crystallizes when the hot solution is cooled.

(iii) ensuring all solid that crystallizes is collected by the filter and not left in the vessel in which the solution was prepared.

(g) M(r) $C_6H_5.COO.CH_3 = 96 + 32 + 8 = 136$

$$2.7\,g = \frac{2.7}{136} \simeq 0.02 \text{ moles}$$

M(r) $HNO_3 = 1 + 14 + 48 = 63$

$$2\,cm^3 = 2 \times 1.5\,g = 3\,g$$

$$3\,g = \frac{3}{63} \simeq 0.05 \text{ moles}$$

(h) Theoretical yield of methyl 3-nitrobenzoate $\simeq 0.02$ mol

M(r) $CH_3.OOC.C_6H_5.NO_2 = 96 + 32 + 7 + 14 + 32 = 181$

$$0.02\,mol = 0.02 \times 181\,g = 0.362\,g$$

Example 19

The flow chart (Figure 32) shows the reaction of some propane derivatives and the diagram in Figure 33 illustrates the infrared spectra of propane and some of the same derivatives.

(a) Compound *Q* gives a positive result with Fehling's solution.

(i) Describe how tests with Fehling's solution are carried out and describe the appearance of a positive result.

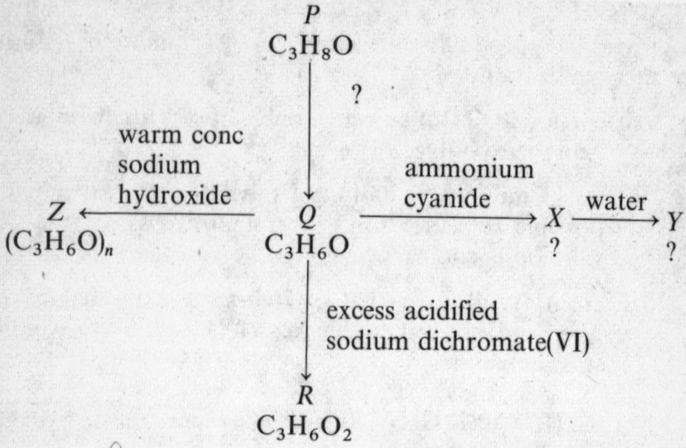

Figure 32

(ii) What is the functional group in *Q*?

(iii) Draw a diagram of the structure of *Q*. 4 *marks*

(b) Compound *P* is readily converted to *Q* in a single stage.

(i) Draw a diagram of the structural formula of *P*.

(ii) Give the name(s) of the reagent(s) needed to convert *P* to *Q*.

(iii) What experimental conditions would you use?

4 *marks*

(c) Compound *R* is weakly acidic.

(i) Draw a diagram of the structural formula of *R*.

(ii) What is the formula of the product of the reaction of *R* with phosphorus pentachloride?

2 *marks*

(d) (i) Suggest, as far as possible, which bonds may be responsible for the peaks in the infrared absorption spectra in Figure 33 at about:

3 μm 3.5 μm 5.9 μm 6.6–7.2 μm

(ii) In the space available in Figure 33 draw the infrared absorption spectrum you would predict for compound *R*. *4 marks*

(e) What *type* of reaction occurs in the changes of *Q* to *Z*? *1 mark*

(f) (i) What is the formula of the product *X*?

(ii) What is the formula of the product *Y*?

(iii) What reagent is used for identification of compounds with functional groups similar to *Y*? *3 marks*

(NUFF)

Answer

(a) **(i)** Equal volumes of Fehling's solutions 1 and 2 [one is copper(II) sulphate solution, the other an alkaline solution of sodium tartrate] are mixed and the carbonyl compound is added. The mixture is heated on a water bath. A yellow-to-pink precipitate of copper(I) oxide is given with carbonyl compounds.

(ii) *Q* contains the aldehyde group

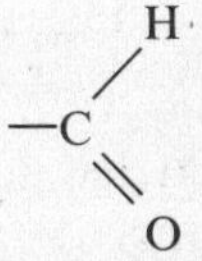

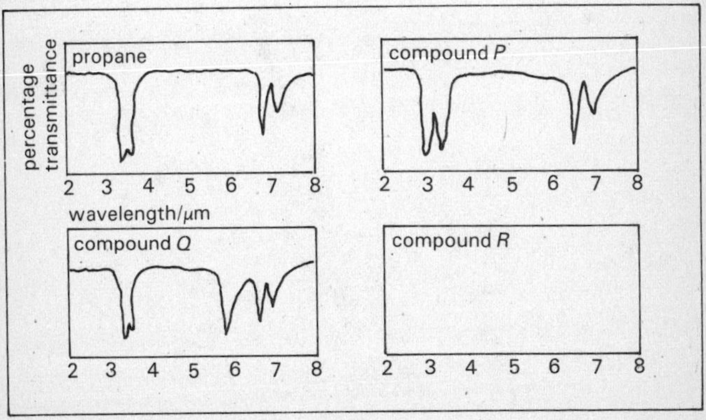

Figure 33

(iii) *Q* is

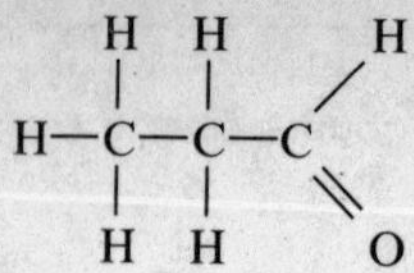

(b) (i) *P* is

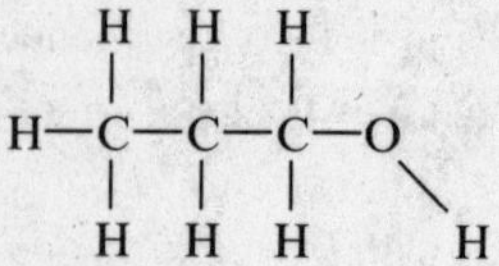

(ii) Acidified dichromate may be used to convert *P* to *Q*.

(iii) Add the acidified dichromate to the propan-1-ol and allow the product to distil, warming gently if necessary.

(c) (i) *R* is

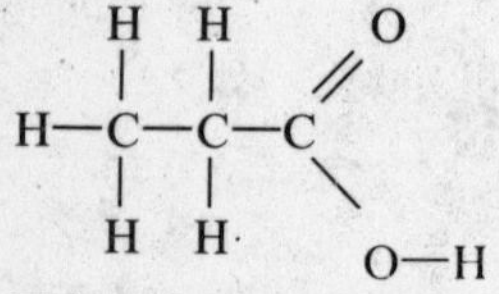

(ii) This gives propanoyl chloride with phosphorus pentachloride:

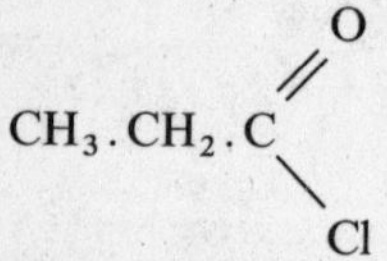

(d) (i) 3 μm: C—OH

3.5 μm: C—C

5.9 μm: C═O

6.6 – 7.2 μm: $—CH_2$ and $—CH_3$

(ii) See Figure 34.

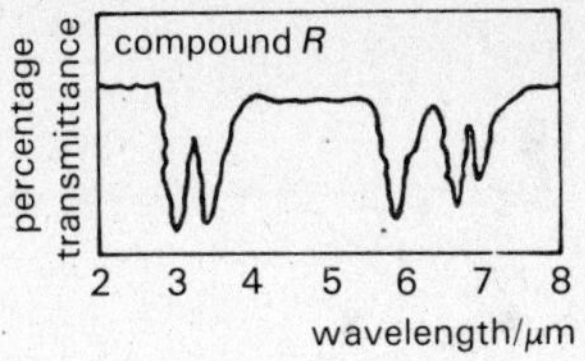

Figure 34

(e) Polymerization.

(f) **(i)** $CH_3.CH_2.\underset{\displaystyle OH}{\underset{|}{CH}}.CN$

(ii) $CH_3.CH_2.\underset{\displaystyle OH}{\underset{|}{CH}}.COOH$

(iii) Iron(III) chloride may be used.

Example 20

(a) How and under what conditions does butylamine react with:

(i) conc hydrobromic acid.

(ii) aqueous copper(II) sulphate.

(iii) ethanoyl chloride (acetyl chloride).

(iv) nitrous acid [nitric(III) acid]?

In each case, indicate the experimental conditions for the reaction, describe what happens, write an equation and give the names and formulae of the reaction products.

20 *marks*

(b) Describe and explain the tests you would perform in order to demonstrate the presence of nitrogen in butylamine.

10 *marks*
(SUJB)

Answer

(a) The formula of butylamine is $CH_3.CH_2.CH_2.CH_2NH_2$.

(i) The amino group is basic, hence the two will react readily to form a soluble salt when the liquid amine is added to the conc aqueous acid:

$$CH_3.CH_2.CH_2.CH_2NH_2 + HBr \rightarrow CH_3.CH_2.CH_2.CH_2NH_3{}^+Br^-$$

The product is butylammonium bromide, a white crystalline solid.

(ii) The nitrogen of the amino group has a lone pair of electrons, which it can denote to electron-pair acceptors. Copper, a transition metal, readily forms co-ordination complexes with donors of this type. If the amine is added to aqueous copper(II) sulphate, a coloured complex will be given. Initially a pale blue ppte of copper(II) hydroxide will be observed as the amine is an alkali: this will be seen to dissolve when an excess of the amine is added:

$$CH_3.CH_2.CH_2.CH_2NH_2 + H_2O \rightarrow CH_3.CH_2.CH_2.CH_2NH_3{}^+ + OH^-$$

$$Cu^{2+}(aq) + 2OH^-(aq) \rightarrow Cu(OH)_2(s)$$

$$Cu^{2+} + 4CH_3.CH_2.CH_2.CH_2NH_2 \rightarrow [Cu(NH_2CH_2.CH_2.CH_2.CH_3)_4]^{2+}$$

Tetrabutylamine copper(II)

(iii) Addition of the ethanoyl chloride to the liquid amine a little at a time will result in a vigorous reaction, the evolution of some hydrogen chloride and the formation of a white solid, *N*-ethanoyl butylamine:

$$CH_3.CH_2.CH_2.CH_2NH_2 + CH_3.COCl \rightarrow$$
$$CH_3.CH_2.CH_2.CH_2.NH.CO.CH_3 + HCl$$

(iv) The amine is dissolved in excess aqueous hydrochloric acid. To this solution, sodium nitrite solution is then added a little at a time. Nitrogen gas will be evolved, the organic product being butan-1-ol:

$$CH_3.CH_2.CH_2.CH_2NH_2 + H^+ + NO_2^- \rightarrow$$
$$CH_3.CH_2.CH_2.CH_2OH + N_2 + H_2O$$

(b) A small piece of sodium should be heated to melting in a hard glass test tube and whilst hot, a little of the liquid amine is added. The tube is heated, gently at first, then more strongly until no fumes are observed. The hot tube is dropped into a mortar containing about 10 cm^3 distilled water, which is covered immediately with a gauze. When reaction has ceased the mixture is well ground and the solution filtered. Some of the filtrate is then added to freshly prepared iron(II) sulphate solution and the mixture heated to boiling. After cooling, the solution is then acidified. A dark blue or green colour may be observed, but if not a little iron(III) chloride is added. As the substance contains nitrogen a dark blue colour will be given.

The heating with sodium reduces nitrogen and carbon in the compound to give sodium cyanide, which is water soluble. On heating this cyanide with iron(II) it forms the complex hexacyanoferrate(II) ion. This, on acidification, reacts with iron(III) ions, some of which may be present due to oxidation of excess iron(II), used to form the complex, to give a dark blue compound. If insufficient iron(II) ions are present, the addition of iron(III) chloride will be required.

Example 21

This question concerns the following aliphatic alcohols:

A $CH_3.CH_2.CH_2OH$

B

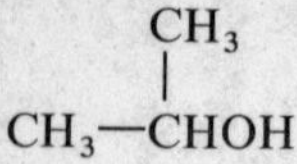

C $CH_3.CH_2.CH_2.CH_2OH$

D

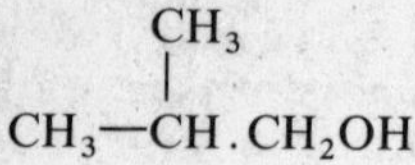

E

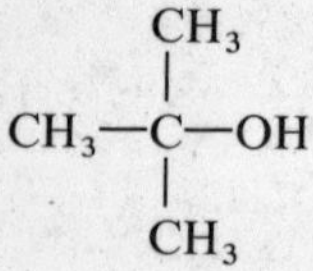

F

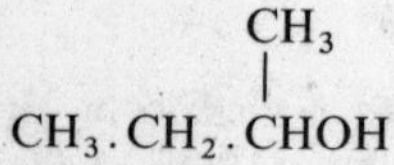

(a) Give the systematic names of *D* and *E*. 2 *marks*

(b) Of the alcohols *A* to *F*, which are primary, which are secondary, and which tertiary? 3 *marks*

(c) How do you account for the fact that the boiling point of *B* is lower than that of *A*? 2 *marks*

(d) Which of the alcohols, *A* to *F*, contain(s) an asymmetric carbon atom? 1 *mark*

(e) Using a different method in each case, describe ONE chemical test to distinguish between

(i) *C* and *F*. (ii) *D* and *E*. 6 *marks*

(L)

Answer

(a) *D* is 2-methylpropan-1-ol.
E is 2-methylpropan-2-ol.

(b) Primary alcohols are *A*, *C* and *D*.
Secondary alcohols are *B* and *F*.
Tertiary alcohol is *E*.

(c) The molecules of both alcohols will be attracted to each other by hydrogen bonding as both contain a polar $-\overset{\delta-}{O}-\overset{\delta+}{H}$ group. An extra attraction in both cases will result from Van der Waals forces, arising due to temporary polarization, which is greater in the primary alcohol

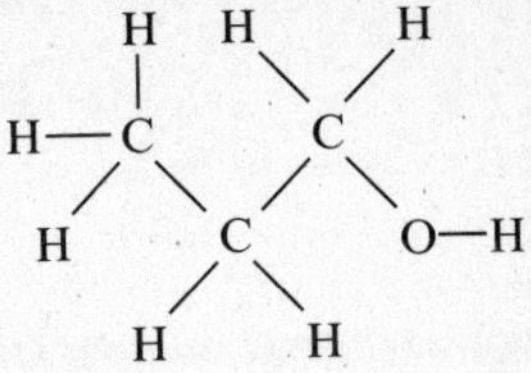

than in the more compact shape of the secondary alcohol

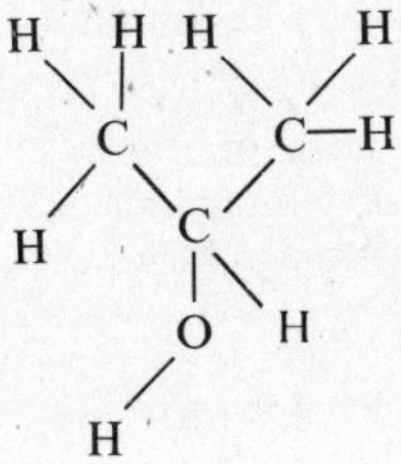

Hence *A* has the slightly higher bp.

(d) *F* contains an asymmetric carbon atom.

(e) (i) *C* and *F* can be distinguished by adding iodine solution, decolorized by addition of dil sodium hydroxide and warming in a water bath. *C* does not react whereas *F*, because it contains an oxidizable $CH_3-\overset{|}{\underset{|}{C}}-O-H$ group, will give a yellow crystalline ppte of triiodomethane.

(ii) *D* and *E* can be distinguished by adding acidified dichromate(VI) solution and warming. *D*, being a primary alcohol is oxidized to the corresponding aldehyde, then the acid, reducing dichromate from its orange colour to give green chromium(III). *E*, a tertiary alcohol, does not oxidize under these conditions, so no colour change will be observed.

Example 22

(a) Chloromethane reacts with an alloy of aluminium and sodium to form the compound *J*.

J has the following composition by mass: C = 50%; H = 12.5%; Al = 37.5%.

0.24 g of *J* react with excess water to produce 0.224 ℓ of the gas, *K*, and a white gelatinous precipitate, *L*.

L dissolves in hydrochloric acid and in sodium hydroxide solution. 25 cm^3 of *K* require 50 cm^3 of oxygen for complete combustion (all gas volumes were measured at stp).

(Relative atomic masses: H = 1.0; C = 12.0; Al = 27.0. Molar volume of a gas at stp = 22.4 $dm^3\,mol^{-1}$.)

(i) Calculate the empirical formula of *J*.
(ii) Suggest a structural formula for *J*.
(iii) Identify the compounds *K* and *L*.
(iv) Write equations for:
the reaction of chloromethane with the Al/Na alloy.
the reaction of *J* with excess water.
the complete combustion of *K*.
the reaction of *L* with hydrochloric acid.
the reaction of *L* with sodium hydroxide solution.

17 *marks*

(b) How, and under what conditions, does bromoethane react with:
(i) potassium hydroxide.
(ii) silver ethanoate (acetate).
(iii) benzene.
Write the equations for the reactions described.

13 *marks*

(SUJB)

Answer

(a) (i) Ratio C:H:Al $= \frac{50}{12} : \frac{12.5}{1} : \frac{37.5}{27}$

[Dividing % by relevant A(r)]

$= 4.17 : 12.5 : 1.39$

$\div$ by 1.39 $\quad = 3:9:1$

Empirical formula of *J* is C_3H_9Al.

(ii) Structural formula for J

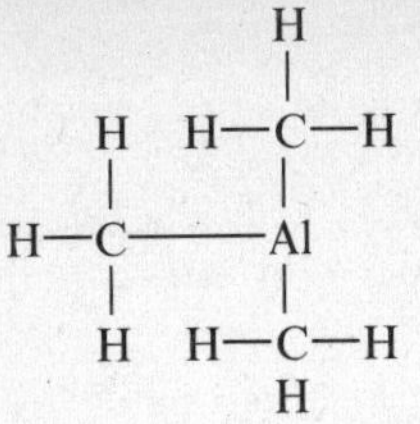

(iii) M(r) $J=(3\times 12)+(9\times 1)+27=72$

$0.24\,g\,J$ on hydrolysis gives $\dfrac{0.224}{22.4}$ moles gas

$72\,g\,J$ on hydrolysis gives $\dfrac{0.224}{22.4}\times\dfrac{72}{0.24}=3$ moles gas

As J contains 3 carbon atoms, each molecule of gas must contain 1 atom of carbon.

K is a hydrocarbon CH_x

$$CH_x+\left(1+\frac{x}{4}\right)O_2 \rightarrow CO_2+\frac{x}{2}H_2O$$

But $25\,cm^3$ K reacts with $50\,cm^3$ oxygen.

1 mol K reacts with 2 mols oxygen.

$\therefore\ 1+\dfrac{x}{4}=2 \qquad \therefore\ x=4 \qquad \therefore\ K=CH_4$

L is amphoteric (it dissolves both in acids and in alkali) and is therefore $Al(OH)_3$ as it must contain the aluminium present in J.

(iv) $3CH_3Cl+3Na/Al \rightarrow 3NaCl+Al(CH_3)_3$

$Al(CH_3)_3+3H_2O \rightarrow Al(OH)_3+3CH_4$

$CH_4+2O_2 \rightarrow CO_2+2H_2O$

$Al(OH)_3+3HCl \rightarrow AlCl_3+3H_2O$

$Al(OH)_3+NaOH \rightarrow NaAl(OH)_4$

(b) (i) Potassium hydroxide can react, under different conditions, to give two different products.

In aqueous solution, the bromoethane would be hydrolysed on refluxing, giving ethanol as the product:

$C_2H_5Br(l)+KOH(aq) \rightarrow C_2H_5OH(aq)+KBr(aq)$

Refluxing with potassium hydroxide in solution in ethanol would result in evolution of ethene, by an elimination reaction:

$$C_2H_5Br + KOH \rightarrow H_2C{=}CH_2 + KBr + H_2O$$

(ii) Silver ethanoate reacts with bromoethane, on refluxing, to give the ester ethyl ethanoate and silver bromide:

$$C_2H_5Br + AgOOC.CH_3 \rightarrow C_2H_5.OOC.CH_3 + AgBr$$

(iii) Benzene reacts with bromoethane when an aluminium chloride catalyst is added and the mixture is refluxed. The product is ethylbenzene:

$$C_2H_5Br + C_6H_6 \xrightarrow{AlCl_3} C_2H_5.C_6H_5 + HBr$$

Example 23

Distinguish between a mono-saccharide, a di-saccharide and a poly-saccharide, giving a specific example of each.

Compare and contrast the reactions of glucose and of starch with

(a) Iodine.
(b) Alkaline Cu^{2+}(aq) (Fehling's solution).
(c) Dilute aqueous sulphuric acid, and
(d) Ammoniacal silver nitrate ('Tollens' reagent').

(L)

Answer

Mono-saccharides are the building units from which other carbohydrates are formed. Most have the general formula $C_nH_{2n}O_n$. An example is glucose, $C_6H_{12}O_6$. They are polyhydric compounds, also containing a carbonyl group $>C{=}0$.

Glucose has the structure (it is one of several isomers):

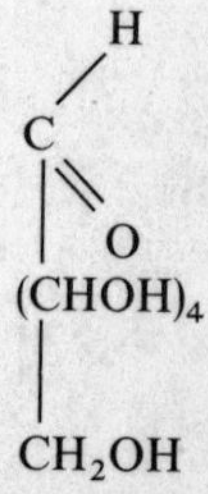

Di-saccharides are the condensation product of the reaction of two mono-saccharides, usually by 1:4 linkage.

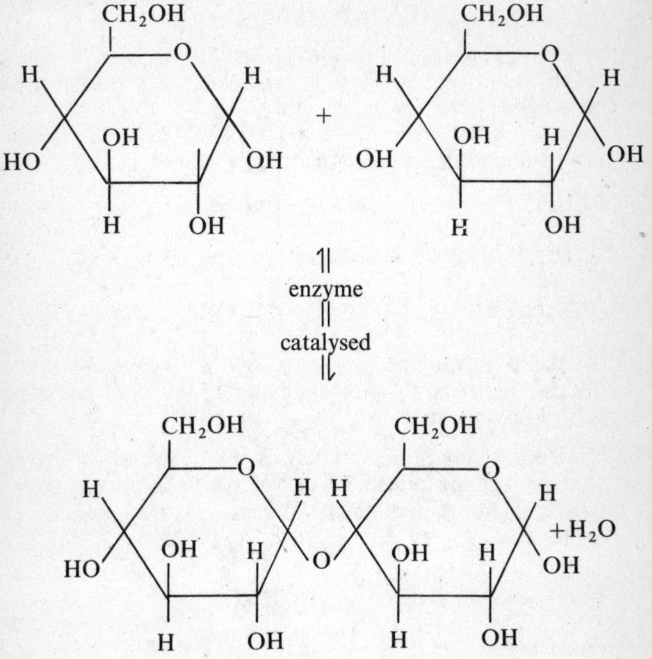

Maltose, $C_{12}H_{22}O_{11}$, is an example of a disaccharide, consisting of 2 glucose molecules linked by the elimination of water.

Polysaccharides consist of many monosaccharide units linked by condensation to give chains and cross linking chains. Starch consists of a large number of glucose molecules, having the formula $(C_6H_{10}O_5)_n$.

$$nC_6H_{12}O \underset{\text{catalyzed}}{\overset{\text{enzyme}}{\rightleftharpoons}} \frac{n}{2}C_{12}H_{22}O_{11} \underset{\text{catalysed}}{\overset{\text{enzyme}}{\rightleftharpoons}} (C_6H_{10}O_5)_n$$

(glucose) maltase (maltose) zymase (starch)

$+ \frac{n}{2}H_2O$ or amylase $+ nH_2O$

(a) Iodine gives a blue black complex with starch, but does not react with glucose. This complex is only a loose combination, but is a useful test for starch as no other carbohydrate gives a reaction.

(b) Alkaline copper(II) solution is reduced by glucose as it contains a free aldehyde group which is oxidized to a carboxylic acid group by this reagent. The copper(II) complex is reduced to copper(I) oxide, obtained as a yellow to reddish precipitate on warming.

$$\begin{matrix} CHO \\ | \\ (CHOH)_4 \\ | \\ CH_2OH \end{matrix} + 2Cu^{2+} + 2H_2O \rightarrow \begin{matrix} COOH \\ | \\ (CHOH)_4 \\ | \\ CH_2OH \end{matrix} + Cu_2O + 4H^+$$

As the aldehyde groups are involved in the bonding of one glucose molecule to another in starch, this does not react with Fehling's solution.

(c) Aqueous sulphuric acid catalyses the hydrolysis of starch and on heating under reflux the starch is broken down giving maltose and finally glucose as the product of hydrolysis.

$$(C_6H_{10}O_5)_n + \frac{n}{2}H_2O \xrightarrow[aq]{H^+} \frac{n}{2}C_{12}H_{22}O_{11}$$

$$C_{12}H_{22}O_{11} + H_2O \xrightarrow[aq]{H^+} 2C_6H_{12}O_6$$

(d) Ammoniacal silver nitrate (Tollens' reagent) is another reagent specific for reducing substances, particularly those containing an aldehyde group. As in (b), the reagent, prepared by adding dilute ammonia solution to silver nitrate solution until the precipitate just dissolves, is reduced on warming in a water bath, when mixed with glucose. The diammine silver(I) complex is reduced to silver which is deposited on the walls of the test tube. Starch does not react for the same reasons as given in (b) above.

Note As starch is hydrolysed to glucose on hydrolysis, eg, with dilute acid, the product of hydrolysis will reduce both Fehling's and Tollens' reagents and will have no reaction with iodine.